I MEET GOD

Through the Strangest People

I MEET GOD

THROUGH THE

STRANGEST PEOPLE

110 Devotions
for the 9 to 13 Generation

Daniel R. Burow

Illustrated by Betty Wind

Concordia Publishing House
Saint Louis   London

Concordia Publishing House, St. Louis, Missouri
Concordia Publishing House Ltd., London, E. C. 1
Copyright © 1970 by Concordia Publishing House
Library of Congress Catalog Card No. 77-98299

MANUFACTURED IN THE UNITED STATES OF AMERICA

Dedication

*To the grandparents
of Mark, Paul, and Betsy*

Contents

You Can Be Great / 13
Though Stained with Tears? / 15
Underneath, the Everlasting Arms / 16
Problems God Can't Handle? / 18
The Monster / 20
Faith That Overcomes / 23
Not Tomorrow but Today / 24
Need a Church Burning? / 26
Driven into Thorns / 28
Stingy Love / 30
When Helping Isn't Fun / 32
Money Greed / 33
Windowless Houses / 35
Bad Luck? / 36
Too Soon, Too Soon! / 38
When Death Strikes / 39
My Lord Would Rather Smile / 42
Cheering for God / 43
No Pretended Love / 45
The Lord's Prayer List / 47
Child on Your Doorstep / 48
Whom Shall We Please? / 50
What's Your Cross? / 52
Kinder to Animals? / 53
The Turning Point / 54
Wind to Heaven / 56
Caught in a Rut / 57

Whose Side Is God On? / 59
Lord of Sun and Snow / 61
Devils in God's House / 62
Our Future Body / 64
Desert Such a Master? / 66
What Makes Forgiving Easy / 68
You May Be Seeing Yourself / 71
What Is Heaven Like? / 72
When School Is Out / 74
Tour with an Angel / 76
Herald at Mrs. Meiners' / 77
Herald and Jesse Blake / 79
Herald at Mr. Oakley's / 81
End of Herald's Tour / 83
Bargain with God? / 84
Made Just Right / 86
Past the Parking Lot / 88
Independence Celebration / 89
One for All / 91
Take Heed How You Hear / 93
A Humorous Situation? / 94
What Price Peace? / 96
Knowledge for Help Power / 98
No Magic Formula / 100
Why Bodies Wear Out / 102
Thanks but No Thanks / 105
The Do-Nothing Sin / 106
Source of All Things / 108
Agent of All Things / 110
Completer of All Things / 111
A Gun at Our Head? / 113
Silly "Cures" / 114
A Guiding Star / 116

Race with Death / 118
People "Read" You / 119
Promise Keeper / 121
Christ's Church for All / 122
No Empty Phrases / 124
Day of Joy / 126
Where Jesus Is Born Today *(Christmas)* / 127
The Beaver's Birthday Party *(Christmas)* / 129
Bridge of Peace / 131
Worse than Worthless / 132
Betrayer Betrayed / 134
Don't Laugh / 137
God's Clearest "Word" / 138
Captain Rogge's Answer / 140
The Enemy Within / 141
Your Voice for God / 143
Visitor from Outer Space / 145
Time's No Cure / 147
Exposed by a Camera / 148
Good from Evil / 151
Life-Saving Ambulance / 153
Return to the Ages *(Ascension)* / 154
Gladdening Those with Tears / 157
My Playground Your Roof / 158
Too Late / 159
Least Likely to Succeed / 161
The Secret of Jesus' Power / 163
Jesus' Brothers and Sisters / 164
Jesus' Own City / 166
Childish People / 167
You're Not Left Out / 169
What a Breakfast Said / 171

Far Removed from Galilee / 173
Tomb Decorators / 174
What Eating an Apple Did / 176
Like a Bulldog / 178
A Quarter May Come Along / 179
Barefoot over Burning Coals / 182
Junk or Treasure / 183
Who Are the Villains? / 185
Poetic Justice / 187
"Where Is His Body?" *(Easter)* / 188
Return of Herald the Angel / 190
Herald and the Poor / 192
Herald and the Discouraged / 193
Herald at the Parsonage / 195
Herald at the Publishers / 197
Herald in the Past / 199
Herald and the Empty Seats / 200
Herald and Stubborn Love / 203

Preface

In his book *The Bridge of San Luis Rey* Thornton Wilder introduces us to Brother Juniper and his unusual experiment. High in the Andes Mountains of Peru Brother Juniper had seen a bridge break, plunging five people to their death.

"Why did this happen to those five?" Brother Juniper wondered. He decided to learn all he could about the lives of those five people. "If I know their lives," he reasoned, "maybe I will also learn why God let them die."

Of course, Brother Juniper's project did not work out. By probing the lives of people we can never discover the hidden secrets of God's will. Some of these secrets God has revealed to us in His Word but nowhere else. And those secrets of His mind which He has not revealed we can never discover. They remain a mystery to us.

Yet in a sense Brother Juniper was right. Through the lives of people we can meet God and get to know Him better. Through people's lives we cannot discover the secrets of God's mind, but we can see God in action loving, caring, forgiving, protecting, correcting, and saving people.

In most of the devotions of this book you will be meeting people—all kinds of people. Some you will recognize, like George Washington and Abraham Lincoln, Mark Twain and Marco Polo. Some may be unfamiliar to you, like Santo Domingo and Maha Vira. Others you

11

can't have known because we made them up, like Herald the Angel and the people he will take you to meet. Some people, like Sydney Carton and Henry Hudson's carpenter, you will admire. Others, like King Xerxes and the sneaky "Cicero," you won't.

Through a great many of these people you will be meeting yourself. In them you will see your own faith and gallantry. You will see also your own weaknesses and worries. But through all these persons it is my hope that you will be introduced to one Person: God, and that in each meeting with Him you will see just how lasting His love for you is.

May this book help you have many inspiring meetings with the Lord, and through these meetings may you receive His power to live your life for Him.

DANIEL R. BUROW

You Can Be Great

BIBLE READING: *Matthew 20:25-28*

What do you want to be when you grow up? President or Prime Minister? An astronaut? A famous actress or doctor?

It would be nice if we could all grow up to be famous or someone very important. But we can't.

A young man, known in history as Santo Domingo, found that out. He lived in Spain way back in the 11th century. More than anything else Santo Domingo wanted to do great things for God, maybe even be a leader of God's people. So he went to a monastery for schooling and training. But the leaders there turned him away.

He tried another monastery. There too he was turned away and for the same reason: he wasn't smart enough. It takes great brains to be a great leader. But he didn't even have the brains to be a little leader.

Santo Domingo now realized that he could never lead people in worship at the great cathedral at Santiago de Compostela. But at least he could help people to get there. The way to the cathedral was very difficult to travel because there were few bridges and at places not even a path. So Santo Domingo went about building footpaths and little bridges for the worshipers.

That's not the kind of work that makes a person great? Not usually; not in the eyes of most people. But it is the kind of thing that makes a person great in the eyes of God. Jesus said: "Whoever wants to be great must be your servant, and whoever would be first must be the willing slave of all—like the Son of Man; He did not come to be served but to serve and to surrender His life as a ransom for many." (NEB)

Maybe we can't all be famous. But what does it matter? We can all do great things. It's as simple as helping a little brother or telling a neighbor about Jesus.

To think about: What have you been doing to serve the people in your family? In what kind of job do you think you can best help others?

Lord Jesus, keep me from complaining about the abilities I don't have. And help me to use the abilities I do have to serve others. Amen.

Though Stained with Tears?

BIBLE READING: *Philippians 4:4-7*

According to an old story from India, there once lived a king who tried to shield his son Gautama from all the unhappiness in the world. He surrounded him with only young, healthy, and happy friends.

But one day Gautama and a young companion sneaked away from the palace. As they wandered the streets of the city, Gautama saw three sights he had never laid eyes on before. They were sick people, old people, and dead people. When his companion told him that sickness, old age, and death happen to people the world over, Gautama said, "Now I can never be happy again."

St. Paul also had discovered how much unhappiness and troubles there are in this world. And he knew we Christians suffer as much as anyone else. Yet he tells us: "Rejoice in the Lord always."

Always? Even when we hurt and when our cheeks are stained with tears? Paul answers: "Again I will say, Rejoice."

Maybe we can't rejoice over our tears or pains or loneliness. But we can always rejoice *in the Lord.* For Jesus, the Prince of heaven, came into this world to share in our kind of life. He was born the way we are born. He experienced loneliness, weakness, and pain just as we do. He died just as all people must die. This is the very reason we can rejoice. By sharing in our troubled life, Jesus made it possible for us to share in His joyous, resurrected life.

So even if we should be surrounded with unhappiness our whole life long, we can still rejoice. For our Lord lives with us, and we shall live with Him forever. Isn't this a joy to conquer all sadness?

To think about: In what ways has Jesus been a joy to you even in times of sadness? In what ways will your joy be even greater when you come to live with the Lord face to face forever?

Lord Jesus, without You pleasures are joyless. But with You, even in sadness I have joy. Give me, O Savior, the joy of Your presence now and forever. Amen.

Underneath, the Everlasting Arms

BIBLE READING: *Deuteronomy 33:26-29*

Paul felt "butterflies" in his stomach. As he looked out the airplane window, he saw the houses below grow smaller and smaller. "This airplane is so big and heavy," he thought. "What if the engines get too tired or weak to keep lifting this load? We'll plunge to the ground like a giant stone." Paul felt frightened and sick.

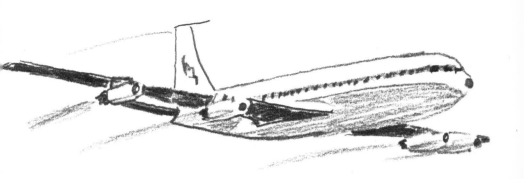

An hour later the stewardess asked him if he wanted dinner. When he answered, "Yes," his father said, "I thought you were feeling sick to your stomach."

"Not anymore," Paul answered. "Those engines have been keeping us up here all this time. I guess they're safe." When Paul learned to trust the plane, his fear and sickness vanished. Now he could enjoy the trip.

At times we may lose our joy in life because we're too afraid of all the things that could go wrong. We may get all tied up in knots worrying about such questions as, "What if I get failing grades in school?" "What if lightning strikes our house?" "What if my parents die?"

God doesn't want us to spend our time fretting. He wants us to put our trust in Him so we can enjoy the life He has given us. To remove our fears, He has made this promise: "The eternal God is your dwelling place, and underneath are the everlasting arms." Sometimes airplane motors fail. But God's powerful arms never tire or fail to support us. Whatever may happen, God assures us: "Even to your old age . . . I will carry you . . . and will save." (Isaiah 46:4)

We can trust our Lord to keep His promise because He has already "borne our griefs and carried our sorrows" all the way to Calvary. After carrying that heavy load for us, surely He will never let us down.

To think about: What things worry you the most? Worrying about things doesn't help us. What does it do to us? Even if some of the things we worry about should happen, what promise do we have from God? How does this help you?

I am trusting Thee, Lord Jesus;
Never let me fall.
I am trusting Thee forever
And for all. Amen.

Problems God Can't Handle?

BIBLE READING: *Isaiah 40:27-31*

Do you sometimes feel that your problems are too big not only for you but also for God?

Thomas Hawkes's friends felt that way. Hawkes, an Englishman who lived about 400 years ago, had been sentenced to be burned at the stake because of his religious beliefs. The day before he was to die, his friends visited him in prison. They were quite worried. For they shared his Christian faith and knew that they too might one day be put to death for their beliefs.

Death itself didn't worry them too much. They knew that for Christians death means to be forever with the Lord. What bothered them was the thought of being burned to death.

"Aren't you afraid?" they asked Hawkes.

"No," he said, "I am sure Jesus will help me bear the terrible pains."

His friends then said, "When you're in the fire, will you give us a signal if God does help you bear the pain?"

"Yes," Thomas Hawkes replied. "I will raise my hands over my head."

The next day as the flames roared up around him, Hawkes slumped forward into the fire. Then suddenly, to everyone's surprise, he straightened up and raised both hands over his head, clapping them together three times. By this signal he showed his friends that God had helped him when he needed it most.

When we need God's help the most, He is there to give it in the way He knows is best. For no trouble

is too big for Him to handle. The bigger our troubles get, the more help our Lord supplies.

The Bible says: "He gives power to the faint, and to him who has no might He increases strength." So when our troubles seem too big, let's not panic but trust in Him who helps in every need.

To think about: What are your biggest problems? Do you think these problems are too big for God to handle? Why or why not?

Tell Jesus your troubles. Ask Him to help you in the way He knows is best.

The Monster

BIBLE READING: *1 John 3:16-18*

Steven Crane's short story "The Monster" is about a Negro man whose face was so badly scarred by fire that people dreaded to look at it. He had received his burns while heroically rescuing his master's son from a burning house.

His master, who was the town doctor, was so grateful that he decided to hire someone to take care of him for the rest of his life. But the scarred man's appearance was so frightening that no one would take the job. So the doctor himself took him into his own house.

The townspeople became angry with the doctor for keeping the man where they might have to look at him. One neighbor moved away. Others refused to go to the doctor anymore. Strangely enough, everyone in town felt sorry for the heroic man, and all agreed "someone" should take care of him. But by "someone" they meant "someone else."

Sometimes we see persons in need of help. We may say or think, "It's a shame about these people. Someone ought to help them." But we wait for someone else to do it.

Can you imagine what would have happened if God had taken such an attitude when He saw us on our way to eternal death? Suppose He had said, "That's too bad. Someone ought to do something, but let someone else do it." Then we would have been lost forever, for there is no one else who can help.

Thank God that He Himself gave us the help we needed. He sent His very own Son to rescue us by dying in our place. Now He calls on us to act in love toward others. The Bible says: "Let us not love in word or speech but in deed and in truth." "In deed" does not mean "let someone else do it." It means for *us* to do it.

To think about: What persons do you know who are in need of help? Is there any way you can help them? Will you? How?

By the way You helped me, O God, teach me to help others. Help me not to count the cost but to be glad that I can show You my thanks by following Your example. Amen.

Faith That Overcomes

BIBLE READING: *1 John 5:1-5*

Some people are able to fight against great odds and win. Alexander the Great was such a man. In one battle his small Greek army was outnumbered more than ten to one by the Persians. Yet Alexander won a great victory.

Later the famous conqueror set out to capture the city of Tyre. People said it couldn't be done. Tyre stood on an island more than a mile off shore, and walls 100 feet high surrounded the city. But in a short time Alexander did capture Tyre as he said he would.

While still quite young, he overcame practically the entire world of his day. How did Alexander do so much with so little in so short a time? For one thing, he believed that he was a god and that nothing could stop him. So he dared great things. His faith in himself —false as it was—gave him great power. But his faith was false! For Alexander was not a god. He died and remains helpless in his grave.

Can you imagine, then, what must be the power of true faith such as we have? Surely with it we can win far greater victories than Alexander did, and against far greater odds.

We can overcome the world Alexander failed to overcome. It is the evil world of temptation and sinful pleasure that surrounds us. It is a world heavily infiltrated with devils and the enormous powers of hell —all seeking to pull us away from God.

Our faith isn't in ourselves but in Jesus, God's Son. And Jesus isn't lying helpless in some grave, like Alexander. He is the living, mighty God, who conquered our enemies for us.

To us who believe in Him, He gives the power to fight against the world and overcome it. The Bible says, "This is the victory that overcomes the world, our faith."

To think about: In whom did Alexander put his faith? In whom is your faith? What can you conquer with your faith that Alexander couldn't with his faith?

Almighty God, give me greater faith in Jesus. And with that faith give me power to defeat everything that tries to keep me from You. Amen.

Not Tomorrow but Today

BIBLE READING: *Matthew 25:1-13*

An elderly pastor told this story in a sermon:

A tourist in Italy went to see a large, beautiful house in the mountains. As he drove up to the house, he noticed how well the lawn, flower beds, and hedges were kept.

The tourist saw no one around except the caretaker. So he asked him, "Is your master at home?"

"No, sir," was the reply.

"When will he return?" the tourist asked.

"I do not know," answered the caretaker.

"Well," said the tourist, "how long has he been gone?"

"Many years," the caretaker told him.

Surprised, the tourist said, "Why, the way you have taken care of his house, one would think you were expecting him tomorrow."

"Not tomorrow but today, sir," said the caretaker, "today!"

By telling this story the elderly pastor was encouraging his people to live each day as if it were the day when they would meet Jesus face to face. The day after preaching this sermon, the pastor himself met Jesus. For the angel of death ushered him into the presence of his Savior.

We never know when Jesus will return for us or when He will call us to meet Him. But each day we have work that He has given us to do. We have lessons to study, parents and family to help, friends to invite to church. If we faithfully do our work, our Lord will one day tell us, "Well done, good and faithful servant."

Jesus wants us to live with Him and for Him now and always. This is why He gave His life for us. And this is why He tells us to be ready always for His return. So like the caretaker in the story, let's expect our Lord not tomorrow but today. Then, whether He comes for us today or not, today will still be a day lived with the Lord.

To think about: Do you honestly expect Jesus to return for you today? How will living each day in expectation of His return make your life different? What can you do to have that kind of expectation?

Lord, make me ready at all times to meet You. For then every day will be lived with You. Amen.

Need a Church Burning?

BIBLE READING: *Psalm 84*

There is a play entitled "The Burning of the Pews." In the play a church burns to the ground. The next day the pastor reads in the paper that several thousand spectators had gathered to watch his church burn down.

The pastor comments, "Think of it! Thousands of people came to watch the pews burn, but not even a few hundred ever came to sit in them."

Why is it that some people will walk miles to see a church burn but will not walk across the street to sit in church? Or why do we who go to church sometimes think the service is boring? Maybe it's because we don't realize what goes on as we sit in the pews.

Perhaps we look at the church service the way we might watch a play. We think all the action takes place up in front. If the pastor puts on an interesting performance, fine; but if not, then we're bored.

But we who worship in church are more than spectators watching a performance. We are the performers, appearing before God. He is the audience. For He meets with us to hear our praises and prayers. But He does more than just look and listen. Through His Word He works in our hearts, drawing us closer to Him.

But we are not in the pews alone. We are placed side by side with other people so we can remind one another of God's love and care for us. We do this, for example, as we sing the hymns together and say the Creed.

When we realize what exciting things happen in the pews, we can say with the psalmist, "I was glad when they said to me, 'Let us go to the house of the Lord!'" (Psalm 122:1). And it won't take a church burning to make us feel that way either!

To think about: If a church service is like a play, what is wrong with thinking that the pastor is the performer and you the audience? In what way is God the audience? the performer? How does your worship help others?

O Lord, help me be glad when I can go to Your house. Let my worship be pleasing to You and helpful to those around me. Amen.

Driven into Thorns

BIBLE READING: *Hebrews 12:5-11*

There was a loud crash of thunder. The sheep became frightened and began to run wildly down the hill. Seeing a large thicket of thorn bushes to their right, the sheep turned left toward the open valley. They did not know that in the valley wolves could easily spot them and kill them.

The shepherd dogs chased after the sheep, barking loudly and trying to stop them from running into the valley. But the sheep kept on. The dogs then began to bite them until finally the sheep turned into the thorn thicket.

Soon the sheep were surrounded by thorn bushes. Every time they tried to scamper away, they got tangled in the thorn bushes. So they soon quit trying. When the shepherd arrived, he rounded up the sheep and led them back up the hill to safety.

The sheep didn't know that the shepherd dogs had saved their lives. They probably thought the dogs were cruel for biting them and driving them into the thorn thicket. But by doing this the dogs had kept the sheep away from the wolves, who would have torn them to pieces.

Sometimes Jesus, our Shepherd, permits us to get hurt or become sick or lonely. Some people think He is punishing us or being cruel when He permits this. But by allowing such things to happen to us Jesus may be turning us from some dangerous path we are traveling.

Jesus simply can't be cruel to us. He loves us too much for that. Remember, He laid down His life for us. Even when He must "discipline" or "correct" us, this too is proof of His love. For the Bible says: "The Lord disciplines him whom He loves." And He does it for our eternal good.

To think about: What is the difference between punishment and discipline? Which of these does God use with you? Why should this make you glad?

Dear Lord, if I should stray from Your path, lead me back again, even if it hurts me. And give me the faith to accept even troubles and pain as a sign of Your love. Amen.

Stingy Love

BIBLE READING: *Jonah 3:10—4:11*

An angry man climbed to the top of a hill and sat down to pout. Before him, as far as the eye could see, spread the city of Nineveh. More than anything else this man wanted God to send fire from heaven to destroy the people of Nineveh. In fact, he was very angry because God had not yet done so. The man's name was Jonah.

Sometime earlier, when Jonah was back in Israel, his own country, God instructed him to go to Nineveh and warn the people of that city that if they did not repent they would be destroyed. When Jonah heard that God might destroy the people of Nineveh, he was delighted. For these people were enemies of Israel.

After first trying to run away, Jonah did warn the Ninevites of God's judgment. But just as he feared, the people repented and asked God to forgive them. And God did forgive them. This is what made Jonah so angry. He even scolded God for being so forgiving and loving.

There are many people like Jonah who want God to be stingy with His love. They want God to love them but not certain other people—their enemies and perhaps foreigners or people of other races. Are you like that? Are there people you'd rather that God didn't love? Do you sometimes wish God would let loose with some divine fireworks on the Soviet Union or the neighborhood bully?

God is most generous with His love toward us—but not only toward us. He gave His Son to die for the sins of all people. That's why He calls on us to be generous in sharing His love.

Jesus said: "If you love only those who love you, what credit is that to you?" (Matthew 5:46 Phillips). Anyone can be stingy with love like that. But it takes a child of God to love as generously and as widely as God does. And that's what you are, aren't you?

Think of people whom you find difficult to love. Ask Jesus to forgive your lovelessness. Ask Him also to love these people and to help you love them also.

When Helping Isn't Fun

BIBLE READING: *Hebrews 12:1-3*

"Dale, didn't you promise to help your teacher set up that display today? It's time for you to be there already."

"Aw, Mom, I was just going to set up my pup tent," Dale argued.

"But you already promised Mr. West."

"I know," Dale groaned. Then, giving the rolled-up pup tent a kick, he said, "But what fun is there in setting up a display?"

"What kind of world would this be if people did only what was fun?" his mother asked.

This question of Dale's mother is worth thinking about. Can you imagine what the world would be like if everyone did only what was fun? There would be a great shortage of food and clothes, houses and stores, cars and bicycles—in fact, of practically everythings you can name. For there are many times when workers don't find it fun to make these things.

Worst of all, there would be no way to heaven, because Jesus would not have come to save us. He didn't get any fun out of trading heaven for a rough manger. Nor did He find it fun to have soldiers pound nails through His hands and feet and put Him to death like a common criminal. The Bible says He hated the shame of dying on a cross.

Why, then, did He go through with it? We know the answer well enough—to redeem us. Just knowing that His sacrifice would redeem us filled Jesus with great joy.

Jesus wants us to help others as He has helped us. We may not always get fun out of it, but we will get something even better—the joy of knowing we are following in His steps.

To think about: Can you think of a time you helped someone even when it wasn't fun? Did helping that person give you a sense of joy? If so, how was the joy better than mere fun?

My Savior, how much You went through to win eternal happiness for me! Give me power to follow Your example and to help others even when it costs me my fun. Amen.

Money Greed

BIBLE READING: *1 Timothy 6:6-11*

The English poet Chaucer once told this story:

During a terrible epidemic many people died. Several drunken men became so angry at death that they said, "Let's go look for Death and kill him."

Everywhere they went, they asked people, "Have you seen Death?" Most people just laughed at them. But after a while the drunks met an old man who said he could help them. He gave them directions to a certain tree not far away. "Under that tree," he told them, "you will find Death."

When the men reached the tree, they saw Death nowhere around, only a large treasure of gold. But once they spotted the gold, their greed made them forget all about their search. Soon they started fighting so fiercely over the treasure that they killed one another. The old man had been right. Under that tree they did find death.

The Bible says: "The love of money is the root of all evil." In itself money can be good. With it we can help the poor, bring offerings to the Lord, and buy the things we need in order to live. But if we fall in love with money — become greedy for it, we will forget all about helping others and also about loving God. Love of money spawns many evils, such as stinginess, worry, fighting, stealing, and even murder.

Greed for money is one of the great temptations the devil uses to destroy people. But our Savior, Jesus, defeated the devil when He died for us and rose again. Because Jesus shares His victory with us, we can overcome even so strong a temptation as greed for money.

To think about: Why do you like money? Have you ever been tempted to do something wrong to get money? How might even the way we spend our money show greed? Why do you want to overcome temptations to greed?

Father in heaven, fill me with such love for You that I will not be lured into loving money instead. Help me show my love for You by the way I get and use money. In Jesus' name I pray. Amen.

Windowless Houses

BIBLE READING: *2 Peter 1:19-21*

Several centuries ago the British government set up a window tax. The more windows a person had in his house, the more taxes he had to pay. So to avoid paying the tax, many people sealed up all their windows or built new houses without windows.

This was a good way not only to keep from paying taxes but also to keep sunlight out of the houses. But what people didn't realize at that time was that sunlight contains valuable vitamins which we need to keep healthy. Sunlight also helps kill many disease germs.

In their windowless houses many people grew weak from lack of sunshine while disease germs thrived. As a result a terrible epidemic broke out in England, and a great many people died.

Each week many people stay away from Sunday school and church. Perhaps they prefer to spend their time sleeping or playing or picnicking. But by making a practice of missing church they are sealing the windows of their heart so the light of God's Word cannot enter.

We all need the light of God's Word even more than we need sunshine. For without that light faith dies. Only God's Word can keep our faith strong and healthy and kill the germs of sin. It does this by strengthening us with the life of Jesus, our Savior.

Keeping the windows of our heart open to God's Word may mean a little less sleep or recreation. But considering the blessings we get from God's Word, it's worth it, isn't it?

To think about: What are you doing to keep the windows of your heart open to God's Word? How has God's Word helped you already? What further help do you need from God's Word?

Thank You, heavenly Father, for giving me opportunities to hear Your Word. Through that Word let Jesus, my Light, shine into my heart. Amen.

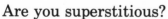

Bad Luck?

BIBLE READING: *Matthew 10:29-31*

Are you superstitious?

Some years ago the TV show "Candid Camera" tried an experiment that proved many people really are superstitious. In a downtown area they opened a large stepladder across a sidewalk. Then hidden cameramen waited to see how people would react to walking under the ladder.

Many people refused to do so. To get around the ladder, they walked out into the middle of the street or climbed over garbage cans. How much easier it would have been to walk under the ladder! But these people were afraid this would bring them bad luck.

It is silly to be superstitious. After all, there is no such thing as luck. God controls everything that happens. Jesus said: "Are not two sparrows sold for a penny? And not one of them will fall to the ground without your Father's will."

To be superstitious is also sinful. For God calls on us to put our trust in Him, not in luck or charms.

Jesus always put His trust in His heavenly Father. He never feared that something evil would happen to Him through bad luck. Even when He faced the cross, His trust never wavered. Our Lord knew that death itself was in His Father's control. And He was sure His Father would use His death to redeem us from sin.

God's Spirit leads us to trust our heavenly Father as Jesus did. He leads us to believe that God loves us and is in control of our lives. When we have such trust, we won't be afraid, even when people try to frighten us with stories about bad luck.

To think about: What things have you been told bring bad luck? Why need you not be afraid of these things?

Lord,
In Thee I place my trust,
On Thee I calmly rest;
I know Thee good, I know Thee just,
And count Thy choice the best. Amen.

Too Soon, Too Soon!

BIBLE READING: *1 Corinthians 10:13*

Many battles are lost because someone gives up too soon. This happened to the British during the Boer War.

The British soldiers charged up Spion Kop, a small hill in South Africa. They hoped to break through the defenses of the Boers, or Dutch farmers, who held the hill. But when they neared the top, they found themselves in a basin with Boer soldiers firing at them from three sides.

The British fought bravely all that day and far into the night but suffered heavy losses. In the hours just before dawn they began retreating down the hill. They had lost the battle. But what they did not realize is that the Boers had also lost many men. And as the British were retreating down one side of the hill, the Boers were retreating down the other side. By dawn not a single soldier of either army was left on the hill. The British could have won the battle without firing another shot if only they hadn't given up so soon.

As we go through life, we often run into temptations that the devil has placed across our path. If we fight the devil and his temptations with the help God gives us, we will win the battle. But if we lose the battle and fall into sin, it isn't because God deserts us. It's because we give up the fight too soon.

By rising from the dead, Jesus proved that He has conquered the devil. Jesus shares His victory with us as we fight against Satan. That's why we can be sure we will win if we do not give up.

To think about: Why did the British lose the battle? Why can you be sure you'll win over the devil if you don't give up?

Ask God for strength to overcome the temptations you meet day by day.

When Death Strikes

Bible Reading: *1 Thessalonians 5:9-11*

A story from long ago tells of a man in India named Gautama. People called him "the enlightened one" because they believed he knew the secrets of their gods.

One day a woman came to see Gautama. She was full of sorrow because her son had died, but she hoped Gautama could give her some comfort. Gautama handed her a large sack and said, "Go throughout the city and gather tiny grains of mustard seed—one from each home in which no one has ever died."

Later the woman returned with the sack still empty. She explained, "I couldn't collect any grain, because at some time in each home someone has died." This was what Gautama wanted her to realize—that everyone else has troubles too. He thought maybe this knowledge would comfort her a bit. It wasn't much comfort, but it was the best Gautama could offer, since he did not know about Jesus.

Through Christ we have a much greater comfort in such times of sorrow. We know that God loves us. He sent His own Son to bear our griefs and carry our sorrows. And He raised Jesus from the dead so that we might have eternal life with Him.

Therefore the Bible promises: "God has not destined us for wrath but to obtain salvation through our Lord Jesus Christ, who died for us so that whether we wake or sleep we might live with Him." This is the good news that comforts us when someone we love dies and also when we must die.

To think about: What thought did Gautama think would comfort the woman? Would such a thought comfort you? What better comfort does God give us through Christ?

Living or dying, Lord,
I ask but to be Thine;
My life in Thee, Thy life in me,
Make heaven forever mine. Amen.

My Lord Would Rather Smile

BIBLE READING: *John 15:12-17*

In recent years artist Richard Hook painted many religious pictures for use in Sunday school lessons. One of his best-known paintings is a close-up of Jesus.

Some people don't like this picture of Jesus. Instead of looking serious, Jesus' face looks lighthearted, his hair uncombed. He looks as if He had just finished playing ball rather than crying over Jerusalem.

Maybe this is the impression the artist wants us to have. For Jesus shares not only in our troubles and sorrows but also in our fun and joy. He is our Friend. So He goes with us when we are romping across the school playground as well as when we are kneeling in church. He is such a good Friend He wants to take part in everything we do—our hymn singing and our party games, our crying and our smiling.

Don't you think Jesus enjoys a good smile? He created the smile. And He has done so much to make us smile. When we are enjoying His blessings and friendship, surely He must smile and His eyes must dance —just as Richard Hook pictures Him.

There are times, of course, when Jesus can't smile. Because He is our Friend, He must be sad when we do or think or say things He can't take part in. When we sin, we leave Him out. And that must make Him very sad. For He knows we are hurting ourselves and possibly some of His other friends as well.

So those people who picture Jesus as being sad may be right. It all depends, doesn't it? Jesus knows how both to smile and to frown. He much prefers to smile, though. Will you give your Friend something to smile about?

To think about: Did you do some things today in which Jesus could not take part? When you are sorry for leaving Jesus out and you ask for His forgiveness, does this make Jesus frown or smile? How will your setting aside regular times for prayer each day help you include Jesus more and more in all you do?

Lord Jesus, I have no other Friend like You. You gave Your life for me. You never tire of forgiving and blessing me. Help me be a better friend to You. Amen.

Cheering for God

BIBLE READING: *Psalm 117*

When Jane came home from the basketball game, she could barely talk, her voice was so hoarse from cheering.

"Why did you cheer so much?" her mother asked.

"I couldn't help myself," was Jane's reply. "The team was doing so well I just had to cheer."

Jane's reason for cheering is something like our reason for worshiping God. We just can't help ourselves. God has done all things so well we can't keep quiet about it.

Our heavenly Father created every tiny detail of this universe. He continues to provide us with all we need to live. Best of all, He has rescued us from our sins. This rescue operation cost Him dearly. He had to give His only Son.

Now through Jesus God adopts us as His children and prepares a place for us with Him in heaven. All this certainly gives us something to cheer about.

Well, that's what worship really is. It's like cheering for God. When we think of all His goodness, we may joyfully sing out, "Hallelujah!" or, "Hosanna!" These are "cheer" words of worship.

Of course, cheering for God may be done more quietly than yelling at a basketball game. Whether our cheers are loud or quiet isn't the important thing. What is important is that we let God and other people hear how wonderful we think our Lord is.

It happens now and then that when worship time rolls around we're not in the mood. Is it because God has quit doing things to cheer about? Hardly! Maybe it's because we haven't thought much about God and what He does. But when we do, we get like Jane again. We just can't help cheering.

To think about: What has God done that makes you most want to cheer for Him?

How wonderful You are, O God! How great is Your love! Help me to praise You in all I do and think and say. Amen.

No Pretended Love

BIBLE READING: *1 John 3:11-18*

Mark Twain had the habit of telling tall stories. One day a friend asked him, "When did you start telling lies?"

He answered, "When I was two months old."

"How can a tiny baby tell a lie?" asked the friend.

Mark Twain explained that a pin in his diaper had come loose and pricked him. When he screamed at the top of his lungs, his mother came running. She picked him up, hugged and kissed him, and spoke soothingly to him.

"The next night I screamed again," Twain said, "but this time I was only pretending."

Pretending can be a way of lying. Very early in life we learn how to pretend. And we usually get better at it as we grow older.

Donald had become an expert at pretending. His mother told him to stop fighting and to shake hands with his brother. Donald shook hands, but he was only pretending. For as soon as his mother left the room, he started fighting again.

At Sunday school Donald's teacher asked, "Do you love everybody?" Donald said, "Yes," but again he was only pretending. He didn't love the neighbor lady who scolded him for cutting across her lawn. And he wouldn't even speak to the new boy at school, because the boy's skin was a different color.

It's easy for us to pretend to love everyone without really doing so. Jesus is the only person who never pretended to love. He said He loved all people, and He proved it by dying on the cross for the sins of the world.

Jesus wants us also to back up our words of love with deeds of love. Through the apostle John He tells us: "Let us not love in word or speech but in deed and in truth." We are to love without pretending, because that's the way Jesus loves us.

To think about: Do you really love everyone, or is some of your love only pretended? How do you know Jesus' love is not pretended?

Lord Jesus, help my love for others to be true, as Your love for me is true. Amen.

The Lord's Prayer List

BIBLE READING: *Matthew 6:7-13*

Have you ever made a prayer list?

Ken made one for the first time in vacation Bible school. He found it such a helpful idea that he now makes one every week. His prayer lists work something like the shopping lists his mother makes out before going to the grocery store. They help him remember all the things he wants to talk to God about.

Writing down a list of things to pray about also gives Ken a chance to ask himself whether the things he prays for are pleasing to God. The first time he examined one of his prayer lists, he discovered his prayers were quite selfish. They showed he thought a lot about himself but little about other people or even about God.

Ken also discovered that he showed far more interest in getting things like clothes or a bicycle than he showed in the spiritual gifts God wants most to give us.

If you examined a list of the things you usually pray about, what would such an examination reveal? Pretty much what Ken discovered about his prayers?

Jesus has made a good prayer list for us. We call it the Lord's Prayer. If we pray for the things on His list, we will avoid being selfish in our prayers. And we will pray more for spiritual blessings such as forgiveness of sins and help in temptation. Remember, it was to win these blessings that Jesus died for us.

47

For your prayer today why not follow Christ's own prayer list? Here it is in modern English:

Our Father in heaven,

1. May everyone honor Your name.
2. Come into our hearts, and rule there as King.
3. Help all of us to do what You want, just as the angels do.
4. Today give me and all people our daily supply of the things we need to serve You.
5. Forgive our sins just as we are forgiving everyone who sins against us.
6. Lead us all away from everything that would cause us to sin.
7. Rescue us from the power of the devil. Amen.

Child on Your Doorstep

BIBLE READING: *John 1:9-14*

The doorbell rang. When Mrs. Tucker opened the door, she heard someone running off around the corner but saw no one. Then at her feet she heard a little cry. Looking down at the doorstep she saw it — a little basket with a baby boy inside.

She didn't know who had left the baby, but whoever it was wanted her to take care of him. Mrs. Tucker did. She took the baby in, fed and clothed him, loved him and raised him as her very own son.

What would you do if someone placed a baby on your steps? In a way someone has. The Bible says: "Unto us a Child is born, unto us a Son is given . . . His name shall be called . . . the mighty God." (Isaiah 9:6 KJV)

God has placed His own Son on our doorsteps. He did so long ago by sending Jesus into our world to live and die for us. But God still sends His Son to us. He sends Him to our homes so He can bring the blessings of forgiveness and eternal life to us and our families.

Some people refuse to welcome Jesus into their home. They offer Him no love. They don't listen to Him and His Word, and they never talk to Him in prayer.

Does your family talk to Jesus? Do you listen together to Him and His Word? Do you show Him love by trying to keep His commandments? Do you honor Him by worshiping Him and speaking highly of Him to others?

If Christ lives in your home as an honored and loved member of your family, your home enjoys a warmth and peace that only God can give. And you know that by His grace one day you will be living with Him in His eternal home.

Dear God, thank You for my family and the love we share with one another. Above all I thank You for the gift of Jesus, who takes away our sins. Help us to honor Him in our home and to give Him the first place in our hearts and lives. Amen.

Whom Shall We Please?

BIBLE READING: *Colossians 1:9-14*

What do you do if a good friend asks you to do something you know is wrong?

To please a friend, Alice passed some answers during an exam. The teacher caught Alice and sent a note to her father. When Alice explained to her father why she had passed the answers, he reminded her of this story:

"A farmer and his son were taking their donkey to town. Because the donkey was old and skinny, neither father nor son rode it. Some people laughed and said, 'Look how stupid they are! With a donkey to ride, they walk.' To please them, the father put his son on the donkey.

"Then some people criticized the son for riding while his father walked. To please them, the son dismounted and the father rode. Farther on other people scolded the father for making his son walk. So both father and son got on the donkey.

"Yet another group of people shouted at them, 'You should be ashamed of yourselves for making that poor animal carry the two of you. You two should be carrying him.' So father and son did just that. But now the donkey was unhappy. As they were crossing a bridge, the donkey kicked wildly and all three fell in the water.

"You see, Alice," her dad continued, "sometimes it is impossible to please everyone. By cheating, you pleased Mary. But you didn't please me or your teacher or God."

There are times when each of us must choose between pleasing people and pleasing God. The Bible encourages us "to lead a life worthy of the Lord, *fully pleasing to Him.*" This is not always easy to do. But because God did not please Himself but gave up His Son for us, we are now His children, equipped with His Spirit. And by the Spirit's power we can make the right choice—to please God.

To think about: When Alice chose to please Mary instead of God, was she really helping Mary? Why not? How does Jesus' life and death show that we help people most by choosing to please God?

Father, help me to please everyone I can, but only if the way I please them also pleases You. Amen.

What's Your Cross?

BIBLE READING: *Matthew 16:24-27*

Boy! I've got problems. I mean like others don't. I like baseball as much as the next guy. And the other guys get to play almost every day after school.

Me? You can see I can't. Who'd take care of little Sis? Dad's gone to heaven. And Mom's at work. You can see Sis needs me. Well, what would you do? Leave her behind, maybe?

Sometimes I think of that. But then I think, "What if Mom left me all alone when I was Sis's age?" Boy, I'd have been scared, really scared. If Mom would walk out on me even now, I don't know what I'd do. She brings home food for me. And gives me her love. The least I can do is take care of Sis for her.

Then I think of Jesus. Boy, what if He went off to play ball that day He was supposed to carry my cross? What a mess I'd be in! Instead of carrying Sis, I'd be carrying my sins around my neck.

So I guess I'll just go on bearing my cross, you know—Sis. Hey, man, what's your cross?

To think about: What crosses does Jesus call on you to bear? Are you bearing them faithfully?

Lord Jesus, I have some jobs I don't enjoy. But it's important that I do them. So help me bear my little crosses as faithfully as You bore my big cross for me. Amen.

Kinder to Animals?

BIBLE READING: *Matthew 25:31-40*

Are you kind to animals?

Maha Vira was. This man, who lived long ago in India, trained himself not to toss in his sleep lest he crush any lice or bedbugs. He believed it was wrong to hurt any living thing, even bedbugs.

Millions of people in India still believe this. So they are very careful not to harm animals. Unfortunately, though, they often fail to treat other people as nicely as they do the animals.

Many people of India are so poor they can't get enough to eat or a house to live in. Yet cows have no such trouble. They are allowed to help themselves to all the food they want in anyone's garden or even in the marketplaces. And when they grow old, some of them are placed into comfortable "nursing homes."

Do you sometimes treat animals better than people? Ron did. He always took good care of his pet dog Rover. But when he saw a small boy fall off a swing at the playground, he just laughed. Once his sister accidentally stepped on Rover's tail. For this he punched her. Ron was showing that he thought more of his dog than of people.

We should be kind to animals. But above all God wants us to be kind to people. Jesus didn't die for animals but for human beings. Our Savior loved us enough to give His life for us. He also wants us to love one another. And He calls on us to show our love by deeds of kindness — especially to people.

To think about: Have you ever been unkind to an animal? Have you ever been unkind to someone in your family? How do you know God wants you to be kinder to people than to animals?

Lord Jesus, help me be kind to other people the way You have been kind to me. Amen.

The Turning Point

BIBLE READING: *Ephesians 5:1-2*

The hero of Victor Hugo's book *Les Miserables* was an escaped convict. He did not hesitate to steal from anyone.

One stormy night a priest welcomed this thief into his home, gave him a meal and a bed to sleep in. The thief repaid the priest's kindness by stealing all his silverware. He didn't get far, though. The police spotted him sneaking off with his sack of stolen goods. He insisted, however, that the priest had given him the silverware. To check his story, the police took him back to the priest's home.

"Is this the way you say 'Thank you'?" the priest scolded the thief. "You sneak away during the night without a word. And so careless too! You took the silverware but forgot to take also the two candlesticks I gave you."

The thief could hardly believe his ears. Instead of having him arrested, the priest was giving him an expensive present. That deed of forgiving kindness became the turning point in the thief's life. He made up his mind to live a new life, to be like that priest — always giving instead of always taking.

Jesus has treated us with even greater kindness. Not only did He refuse to punish us as we deserve; He gave up His life so that we might have God's forgiveness. Jesus' act of kindness has become the great turning point in many people's lives. It has changed them into people who want to be like Jesus.

This is the way God wants it. St. Paul writes: "Be imitators of God as beloved children. And walk in love as Christ loved us and gave Himself up for us."

Do you want to be like Jesus — kind, loving, and forgiving? You can be. Just remember Jesus' great act of kindness toward you. Remembering this has power to help you live the Christlike life.

To think about: The thief in Victor Hugo's book kept the silver candlesticks as a constant reminder of the priest's kindness. What can you use to keep on reminding yourself of Jesus' great kindness toward you?

My Savior, You suffered what I deserved. Help me remember Your kindness always. And help me be more and more like You. Amen.

Wind to Heaven

BIBLE READING: *Galatians 5:16-26*

Hurricane winds were battering the closed shutters of the living room window. Andy was a bit frightened, though he tried not to show it.

Turning to his father, he asked, "Why did God have to create the wind, Dad?"

"You mustn't think all winds are bad," his father replied. "Some winds bring us cool breezes on hot summer days. Some bring rain clouds that water the earth. Some blow the pollen that fertilizes the blossoms of plants and trees. You see, there are different kinds of winds. Some may destroy, but others help us a great deal. In fact, without them life would be impossible on this earth."

A spirit is very much like wind. The wind moves clouds and leaves. So spirits often move us to do the things we do. But just as there are good and bad winds, so there is a good spirit, and there are bad spirits.

The evil spirits are the devils. They destroy by moving people away from God and toward hell. The good spirit is the Third Person of the Trinity. He is God. We call Him the *Holy* Spirit because He helps us do the things that are pleasing to God.

The Holy Spirit came to us in Baptism. He causes us to believe in Jesus, who took away our sins. And just as a good wind moves a sailboat to its harbor, so the Holy Spirit moves us back to God.

He does this through His Word. This is why hearing the Word of God regularly is so important. Then the Holy Spirit can keep us close to God, no matter how strongly the evil spirits try to move us away from Him.

To think about: Why do we call the Holy Spirit "Holy"? What evidence of His work do you see in your life?

Lord God, thank You for the good winds that make life pleasant. And thank You especially for the Holy Spirit, who helps me reach my home above. Amen.

Caught in a Rut

BIBLE READING: *Ephesians 4:22-32*

Did you ever get caught in a rut? The Perkins family did.

When they reached the fork in the old dirt road, Mr. Perkins tried steering the car to the right. But it kept going left. Mr. Perkins stopped and got out.

After examining the situation he told his family, "We're caught in our own rut. All during the school year we always turned left here to take Peter to school. Each day I guess our wheels dug the rut a bit deeper. Now it's so deep the wheels just follow it automatically. That's why we turned left although I steered to the right."

Habits are very much like ruts. Every act we do leaves an impression on our brain the way car tires leave an impression on a muddy road. Each time we repeat the act, the impression sinks deeper. Finally we begin doing the act automatically. When this happens, we have formed a habit.

That's why it is so important to break bad habits early. We may tell ourselves, "I'll break my bad habits later." But the longer we wait, the deeper the habits get, and the harder they are to get out of.

It is true that when Jesus died on Calvary He won forgiveness for all our sins, including the sins we commit out of habit. But as children of God we don't want to use God's forgiveness as permission to continue in our bad habits. Our bad habits hinder our lives from giving glory to God. They may also steer us away from faith in Jesus and the road to eternal life. So let's make every effort to break bad habits *now*.

If now is the best time to break bad habits, it is also the best time to form good ones. The earlier in life we form them, the deeper they will be later on and the harder to break. This is why the Bible tells us: "Remember also your Creator *in the days of your youth*." (Ecclesiastes 12:1)

To think about: What bad habits would you like to break? What good habits would you like to form? Why would daily Bible reading be a good habit to form?

My Father, help me begin today to break my bad habits and to form more good ones. Amen.

Whose Side Is God On?

BIBLE READING: *2 Corinthians 5:14-21*

The movie *The Longest Day* is about the Allied invasion of France during World War II. In one scene an American general receives the news that the invasion may have to be postponed because of stormy weather. The general says in disgust, "Sometimes I wonder whose side God is on!"

In another scene, shortly after the invasion takes place, a German general phones Hitler for permission to use reserve troops to launch a counterattack. But

59

he is told, "Hitler has taken a sleeping pill and cannot be disturbed."

The angry general mutters, "The fate of Europe is being decided by a sleeping pill. Sometimes I wonder whose side God is on!"

Whose side *is* God on? When we're in an argument or have a difference of opinion with someone, we may think: "God is on my side." But God doesn't choose up sides. He is on everyone's side, whether they are our friends or enemies, whether they are of our race or not, or whether they are from our country or another.

To show that He is on the side of all people everywhere, Jesus befriended the rich and the poor. He helped His friends and His enemies, the good and the bad, those in the right and those in the wrong. And finally Jesus died "not for our sins only but also for the sins of the whole world" (1 John 2:2). Because He died for all, we know He is on everyone's side.

The real question is, "Are we on God's side?" We are when we believe in His Son as our Savior and King. And when we are on God's side, we try to lead others, too, to be on His side through faith in Jesus.

To think about: How do you know God is on your side? How do you know you are on His side? How can you help others be on His side too? Are you doing this? Will you?

Dear Father, help me and everyone else to be on Your side, just as You have been on everyone's side all along. Amen.

Lord of Sun and Snow

BIBLE READING: *Psalm 147:7-18*

What do you do when you don't like the weather? Here is what Xerxes (ZURK-seez) the Great, king of Persia, did.

Xerxes was leading his armies in an invasion of Greece. But separating him from his goal was the Hellespont, a narrow body of water between Asia and Greece. His engineers tied many boats together to form bridges across the Hellespont. But before the Persian soldiers could cross, a violent storm destroyed the bridges. Xerxes became so angry at the sea that he ordered his soldiers to give it 300 lashes with the whip.

Even when a late winter storm kills our flowers or a sudden thaw forces us to cancel an ice-skating party, we wouldn't be so foolish as to spank the snow or scold the sun. But we may complain about the weather. And when we do that, we're really complaining against God. For it is He who makes the weather. The Bible says about God: "He gives snow like wool; He scatters hoarfrost like ashes. He casts forth His ice like morsels. . . . He sends forth His word and melts them."

Certainly we don't want to be grumbling against God. That would be not only sinful but foolish, because God always knows what is best for us. For example, when He caused the weather to destroy Xerxes' bridges, He had really done Xerxes a favor. Xerxes discovered this later when he finally got some bridges built and crossed over into Greece. For there the Greeks severely defeated his armies.

The weather is one of the blessings God gives the world. Through it He provides food for man and beast. Even when the weather seems hurtful, God brings good out of it for those who love Jesus. The Bible promises: "All things work together for good to them that love God" (Romans 8:28 KJV). "All things" includes also the weather.

To think about: What kinds of weather do you like least? Even though you may not understand how, why can you be sure God can use even the worst of weather to do you good?

Father in heaven, teach me to thank You for the weather instead of complaining about it. Because You love me in Christ, my Savior, I believe that You govern also the weather for my good. Amen.

Devils in God's House

BIBLE READING: *Ephesians 6:10-13*

In India some men were leading an elephant out of a large Hindu temple. The elephant was nearly covered with ornaments and jewels. But the elaborate howdah, or seat, on top of the elephant was empty.

A man in a tour bus driving by asked the guide, "Who's supposed to ride that elephant?"

"The devils," the tour guide answered. "You see, some Hindus think that if they dress up the elephant this way, the devils inside the temple can't resist taking a ride on it. Did you notice that as soon as the elephant was outside, the people inside the temple quickly closed the doors? They believe that now they've got the devils locked outside while they worship inside."

How foolish for people to believe they can outsmart the devils! The devils were once angels of God and are still much smarter than any human being. They follow us everywhere we go, even when we enter God's house for worship. In fact, when we're at worship, they use every possible trick to keep us from putting our heart into our prayers and praises. They also try to keep us from listening to God's Word. If they fail in that, they tempt us to disbelieve or disobey it.

No elephant trick or anything else we may try can stop the devils. But Jesus can. He proved His power

over them when He died on the cross and rose again. In Jesus, then, we have a strong Conqueror who can help us resist the devils and their temptations. He can keep them from robbing our hearts of God's saving Word.

So when we enter God's house, let's remember to ask Jesus for His help. That's far more effective than locking the church doors behind us.

To think about: Think of your own experiences. How can you tell that the devil is with you even in God's house? What can you do to resist the devil?

Lord, be with me when I enter Your house. Help me overcome the tricks of Satan. Make the words of my mouth and the meditation of my heart acceptable in Your sight, for You are my Strength and my Redeemer. Amen.

Our Future Body

BIBLE READING: *1 Corinthians 15:35-50*

The Pattersons were seated around the supper table having family devotions. This evening they were discussing the meaning of Easter. Ron seemed troubled. He asked, "Dad, when Jesus raises my body from the dead, will it be the same as it is now?" Ron had lost one eye in a sledding accident.

His father went to the kitchen and came back with the window box and a package of petunia seeds. "Remember how we planted tiny seeds like this in the window box?" he asked. "But look. Now they've been transformed into green plants with stems and leaves. Soon they'll have bright, pink flowers too. The plants are far more wonderful than the seeds from which they came.

"The Bible tells us that when God raises our bodies from the grave He will transform them into bodies far more wonderful than we now have. They will have power to do things we can't even imagine now. Listen to what the Bible says: 'Just as we have borne the image of the man of dust, we shall also bear the image of the man of heaven.' There will be nothing at all wrong with our new bodies."

"But didn't Jesus' resurrected body still have nailprints in it?" Ron asked.

"That's true," his father said. "But He probably kept those only to convince His disciples that He was the same Jesus who had been crucified. His resurrected body is a very glorious body, surely the best body that God can make. And the Bible tells us we will have bodies like His."

"As good as His?" Ron smiled. "Well, that's plenty good enough for me!"

"And that promise isn't only for you, Ron," his mother chimed in, "but for all who believe in Jesus."

To think about: According to the Bible reading why must our resurrected body be different from our present body? In what ways will it be changed? Does this make you glad? Why?

Ever-loving Savior, help me always believe in You that I may someday rise from the dead and live with You in a glorious body like Yours. Amen.

Desert Such a Master?

BIBLE READING: *Revelation 2:10-11*

Henry Hudson had already discovered the great bay that bears his name. But ice had trapped his ship in the bay for so long that the food supply was now dangerously low.

One Saturday the crew mutinied. They put Hudson, his son, and a few sick sailors in a little boat. As the crew was about to sail away, the ship's carpenter climbed over the side to join Hudson in the little boat.

"But you can stay with us," the crew told him.

The carpenter answered, "I'd rather trust myself

to the mercy of God and stay with my dear master than be safe and warm with wicked companions like you."

The crew cut the little boat free and sailed away, leaving Hudson, the carpenter, and the others all alone in the great frozen north. What happened to the men in the little boat? No one knows. They were never heard from again.

Sometimes we are forced to make the same kind of choice the carpenter had to make. We can remain faithful to Jesus, our dear Master, or we can join our companions in doing wicked things. The choice is not easy. If we refuse to join our friends in stealing or using bad language or other evil deeds, they may no longer want us for friends.

Which do you choose? A psalm writer once said: "I would rather be a doorkeeper in the house of my God than dwell in the tents of wickedness" (Psalm 84:10). But we don't always choose that way, do we?

Yet here we see what a dear Master we have. Though we desert Him, He promises: "I will never leave you or desert you" (Hebrews 13:5 NEB). He chose rather to give up His life than to leave us in the lurch. And He forgives even our unfaithfulness. Can we desert such a Master?

To think about: What added encouragement to being faithful does Jesus give us in today's Bible reading?

Dear Master, I'd rather have the joy of Your company than all the thrills that wickedness offers. But I am so weak and sinful I need Your help. Help me be faithful to You. Amen.

What Makes Forgiving Easy

BIBLE READING: *Matthew 18:21-35*

Do you find it hard to forgive someone who has wronged you? It can be easy, as Frederick the Great discovered.

Frederick's father was a very strict king. He put people to death for the least little crime. Once a man who had stolen twelve dollars to buy his family some food begged the king for forgiveness. The king ordered the man hanged.

Frederick tried to escape from his father's kingdom. He talked a young army lieutenant named Katte into helping him, but the two of them were caught and thrown in prison. Frederick, of course, was not put to death, because he was the king's son. But when he saw his friend being led to execution, he cried out, "Oh, my dear Katte, I beg a thousand pardons."

Katte replied, "Master, there is nothing to forgive."

Frederick knew there was much to forgive. His foolish adventure was costing Katte his life. But he also knew that his friend had already forgiven him. That's what made the big change in Frederick's life. From that time on he became a forgiving man. And when he became king, he did away with a great many of the harsh punishments his father had used.

Shouldn't it be as easy for us to forgive others as it was for Frederick? We too have been forgiven, yet not for one foolish adventure but for all our sins. Our sins cost Jesus His life. Yet God forgives us. In fact, Jesus could have escaped. Instead He went to His death without struggle or protest. In this way He wanted to show us that all is forgiven.

Can we see how much we've been forgiven and still be unforgiving? Yes, it's possible. But it's pretty hard. A good, long look at God's forgiving us makes forgiving others the only easy thing.

To think about: What makes it easy for us to forgive others? If we find it hard to forgive others, what do we probably fail to realize?

Heavenly Father, remind me of how much You forgive me every day. For then only can I truly forgive others in my heart. Amen.

You May Be Seeing Yourself

BIBLE READING: *Leviticus 19:32*

Hello. Do you think a wrinkled old woman like me looks funny? *Some* young folks think so. I used to think so too—back when I was young.

Well, that's one thing I wanted you to know: I was young once. The way I look now I guess you thought I came from another planet. But once upon a time I was like you—smooth and shiny new. When I saw people with wrinkles and gray hair and a crooked back, sometimes I laughed at them. And sometimes I called them "old man" or "wicked old witch."

Now I'm sorry, because I know how they must have felt. You see, some young people now call me those same old names.

That leads me to the second thing I wanted to tell you. When you look at me, you may be looking at yourself. Because you may look like this someday—unless Jesus comes first or you die first.

You see, when you think of growing up, you think of growing bigger and stronger. But you don't just get bigger. You also grow older—older and older, until one day you're wrinkled and gray and weak like me.

I'm not trying to frighten you. Really it's not so bad being old. I find it difficult, of course, when young people laugh at me. But Jesus loves me and cares for me just as much now as He did when I was young. So I know He'll keep on loving you even when you're old.

But if you remember that you may be old someday, maybe you'll feel more kindly toward us who are already old. And maybe you'll even say a prayer for us. Will you?

To think about: What special problems do old people have? What problems do you think you'll have if and when you become old? What old people do you know? How can you make life more pleasant for them?

Prayer suggestion: Ask the Lord to help the old people you know. Ask Him also to help you do things that will make life more pleasant for them.

What Is Heaven Like?

BIBLE READING: *Revelation 21:9-21*

Since we hope to live in heaven, it is only natural that we should be curious to know what it is like. But the Bible doesn't give us many descriptions of heaven. Why this is so we may better understand if we recall the experience of Marco Polo.

About 700 years ago Marco Polo traveled to far-off China. There he saw wonderful palaces and cities beyond anything he had ever dreamed possible. And for the first time he saw such things as silk, paper, firecrackers, and a compass.

After many years he returned to his homeland in Italy. There he wrote a book about the places he had been and the things he had seen. When people read the book, they said it was nothing but wild and fantastic tales. You see, these people had never been to that part of the world. And they just couldn't believe that such things could really be true.

Later, when Marco Polo was dying, people asked him, "Were you really telling us the truth?"

He answered, "I never told the half of it!"

In fact, Marco Polo *couldn't* describe everything he saw. For some things were so different from what people in Europe knew about that he couldn't even find words to describe them.

If a person came back from heaven, he would have the same problem. Heaven is so much more wonderful than anything we are familiar with on earth that he wouldn't know how to describe it to us.

The best the Bible writers could do was to get us to think of the most beautiful things we can imagine. To some this may be golden streets, a crystal sea, and gates of pearl. Maybe your imagination suggests even better pictures. Whatever our pictures, the Bible writers would say: "Well, something like that, only that isn't even the half of it!"

Whatever heaven is like, we will love it. And best of all, Jesus, who made it all possible, will be there with us.

Lord God, for the promise of heaven I thank You. Keep me faithful to You so I will not lose this precious gift. For Jesus' sake. Amen.

When School Is Out

BIBLE READING: *Psalm 1*

"June is busting out all over!" So goes a line from a well-known song. When school days are over, maybe that is what we feel like doing — "busting out" and getting away from it all, from schoolrooms and teachers, homework and books. We all need a vacation. Even Jesus needed times to get away and relax.

Getting away is fine as long as we don't get away from it *all*. Some things we dare not get away from — like those safety rules we learn at school. We don't want vacation time to be our time for a serious accident.

We don't want to get away from being the kind and helpful person Jesus taught us to be.

And certainly we don't want to get away from God. We can't, of course. But why even try? Who is a better Friend? Who can give us more happiness than He who gave His Son's life to bring us eternal joy? So when vacation days are here, let's remember to keep church and Sunday school, prayer and devotions in our plans.

If you go somewhere on vacation, leave your arithmetic and spelling books behind if you like. But how about taking your Bible with you? It's a book, yes, but one we never want to get away from. For one thing the Bible reminds us that God never takes a vacation from us. He doesn't close down His love and care for a season so He can get away from us for a while. If He did, that would be the end of us.

God, who takes no vacations, is the inventor of vacations. He invented them just for us — another sign of His love. So let's enjoy the vacations He gives us. But let's vacation with God, not from God.

To think about: What plans have you made for your summer vacation? How can you include God in your plans?

O loving Lord, be in my vacations — in every stroll I take and every scene I see, in every thought I think and every page I read. Amen.

Tour with an Angel

BIBLE READING: *Matthew 13:31-32*

You probably don't know me. My name is Herald.
I'm an angel, but don't let that scare you. C'mon. I want
to show you something. It's a story many people don't
know about.

Let's start at the beginning where most good
things begin—at church. Now, I can guess what you're
thinking: "What good ever starts at church?" Lots of
people ask that, more so today than before. Some say
there's nothing but hypocrites at church, hypocrites
and a lot of cheap talk. Well, c'mon. I want to show you
some things most people never see.

Here we are. Recognize that man in the pulpit?
He's your pastor. And I guess you recognize most of
the people, even if you don't know many of them by
name. But listen. The pastor is saying something
I want you to hear.

"Jesus suffered for us, leaving us an example
that we should walk in His steps. His love and sacrifice
have saved us from our sins. And our love and concern
can save so many people from their misery."

That's enough for now. Sounds like the same old
stuff, doesn't it? Just talk! But look around for a minute.
What you see here are the people of God. And by that
"old stuff" you heard, God has just reached down and
stirred some of His people. Take Mrs. Meiners there—
the one with those long, silly gloves and that big hat

76

that always blocks your view. That talk you just heard won't be talk long. It started something going in her and in some others too.

If you'll stick with me for a couple of days, I'll show you what I mean. Just remember, when God's Word meets God's people, things happen — things the world often knows nothing about. See you tomorrow?

To think about: Do you sometimes think that nothing really important happens in church? If so, take this tour with Herald. He'll have some surprises for you.

Lord God, help me realize the importance of Your Word in my life. And make it a power for good within me. Amen.

Herald at Mrs. Meiners'

BIBLE READING: *Matthew 6:1-4*

Hi! It's Herald the angel again. I hope you don't mind going along to visit Mrs. Meiners' house today. It's a run-down place, but she's a widow with no husband to make the repairs. You remember Mrs. Meiners, don't you — the lady you saw in church yesterday with the big hat and long, silly gloves? Funny thing, she knows the hat's too big and the gloves old fashioned. But she doesn't have money for new clothes — just enough for food.

There she is trying to read the newspaper. The print's all a blur. Her eyes really aren't bad, though. They're just filled with tears. You see, she just read about a family that lost its baby and everything it owned in a fire. She's trying to make out the address where the family is staying now. Watch what she does.

See? She's taking that 10-dollar bill out of the cookie jar. That's her food money for the week. And she's mailing it to that family. Oh, there'll be some hungry nights in this house this week. You know why she's doing this? Because of what she heard in church yesterday. She can't remember the exact words. But she has a picture in her mind of Jesus dying on the cross for her. Now she wants to make some little sacrifice to help someone else.

In next week's newspaper you'll see a letter someone will write to the editor. It will praise the news-

paper for the hundreds of dollars, food packages, and bundles of clothing the paper raised for that needy family. Lots of people will praise the newspaper. But you won't hear a word about Mrs. Meiners and many others like her who remembered Jesus and sent in those dollars and bundles. That's the kind of thing sometimes only God and we angels know about.

I'll show you some more things that began in church Sunday, but let's wait till tomorrow. OK?

To think about: Do you know of some kind deeds God's Word has inspired, but they have never been written up in the newspaper?

Father in heaven, thank You for the many people Your Word quietly inspires to make ours a better world to live in. Amen.

Herald and Jesse Blake

BIBLE READING: *Hebrews 13:1-3*

I notice you're not afraid of angels anymore. Good. Let's hurry and get in the back seat of this car. Here comes Jesse Blake. We'll ride home with him from work tonight. I don't want you to miss this.

I'll bet you didn't know him in his overalls. In church he's the one who always wears a baggy gray suit.

Now watch carefully along this deserted stretch of road. There—in the headlights! See that man lying at the side of the road behind the parked car? That man needs help. Or it could be a trick—robbers hiding in the darkness. That's what Mr. Blake is thinking right now. Should he take a chance and stop? He's got a wife and children to think of, you know.

Ah, but see, he's slowing down. He's going to stop because he's also thinking about how Jesus helped him. He's going to run the risk because of what the pastor said Sunday.

It *is* a trick! They've got guns. But don't get scared; they can't see us. Ouch! Poor Mr. Blake. That was a nasty knock on the head. Let's hurry and get out of the car before they drive off with it.

Don't worry about Mr. Blake. A day in the hospital and he'll be OK. But he's out one car and all the money he was carrying.

You know what people will call Mr. Blake for this? A hero? A good Samaritan? No, a fool! They'll say he should never have taken the chance. But Mr. Blake will know better. After all, it *could* have been a person in trouble. Besides, if no one took chances in helping people, how many thousands of needy people would never be helped!

Mr. Blake remembered that Jesus gave His life for him. So he thought the least he could do was risk his life to help someone else.

To think about: According to the Bible reading whom might we be neglecting if we fail to help a person in need?

80

Dear Father, help me remember that Your kind of love is willing to run risks to help people. Fill me with Your kind of love. Amen.

Herald at Mr. Oakley's

BIBLE READING: *1 Timothy 2:1-4*

Getting a bit tired of your tour with an angel? One more stop, OK? I want you to see Mr. Oakley tonight.

Quite an estate he has, huh? Well, he has more money in the bank than you'll see in a lifetime. But he helps a lot of people with his money.

Right now he's got a problem money won't solve. Remember that announcement in Sunday's bulletin— the one about poor Mrs. Owens being in the hospital in critical condition? Mr. Oakley barely knows Mrs. Owens, but he wants to help. He'd write a big check if it'd help. But it won't. She's in God's hands now.

There! He's looking at the clock. He's due at an important meeting, but see, he's going into his study to pray. Watch the clock. Two minutes, three minutes, five minutes. Now he's done—for the moment. Five minutes praying for a lady he hardly knows! Did you know Mr. Oakley can make $1,000 in 5 minutes? His time is valuable.

Some people would say he was wasting valuable time praying for Mrs. Owens. They say no one can change God's will anyhow. And in a way they're right. God wills to do nothing but good for Mrs. Owens and all His people. He won't let anyone change His mind about *that!* Yet God has many ways to do good to Mrs. Owens whether she lives or dies. And in what *way* He'll show good to Mrs. Owens is the kind of decision He often makes after hearing the prayers of His children.

I'll let you in on a little secret. God heard Mr. Oakley before, when he was pouring out his heart for Mrs. Owens. And God is going to make Mrs. Owens well again. He can't always do as His children ask, because He knows sometimes it would turn out badly. But what I really wanted you to know was what Mr. Oakley was doing. And it all started in church with just that little reminder about what Jesus has done for Mr. Oakley and you.

To think about: Do you spend time praying for other people?

Lord Jesus, thank You for giving me many opportunities to help people through prayer. Help me use these opportunities. Amen.

End of Herald's Tour

BIBLE READING: *1 Corinthians 15:58*

It's me again—Herald, the angel. I hope I'm not pestering you, but something's come up I just had to share with you. Will you make a quick trip with me to your pastor's office? Good. Let's go.

Here we are. Now look at all the wastepaper on the floor beside his desk. Your pastor's having a rough time preparing his sermon for Sunday. Maybe you didn't know. Maybe you thought he just got up in the pulpit and started talking. No, your pastor spends many hours each week preparing sermons.

But notice the wrinkles in his brow. He's feeling mighty discouraged right now, and it's not the first time. He feels he's not getting God's message through to people. Did you know he's thinking of giving up being a pastor? That's right. He feels he's a total failure, that his sermons aren't making any difference in people's lives.

Well, you know yourself he doesn't always get through to people. Right? Remember the times you couldn't make heads or tails of what he was driving at, so you just quit listening?

Trouble is he doesn't see what we angels see and what you've seen with me these past few days. And what's worse, most of the time people don't tell him how his preaching and teaching of God's Word have made a difference in their lives.

Now I'll take you back home. But will you do me a favor? Next time your pastor says something that strengthens your faith or makes your love glow or stirs you to action, will you tell him? Maybe when you leave church you can just shake his hand and say, "Thanks." He'll know what you mean.

St. Paul once encouraged God's people by writing: "Be steadfast, immovable, always abounding in the work of the Lord, knowing that in the Lord your labor is not in vain." It'd be so nice if God's people would also give that kind of encouragement to His ministers. Well, thanks for coming with me. Good-bye.

To think about: In what ways has your pastor been an encouragement to you? How can you be an encouragement to him?

Dear Jesus, help me be an encouragement to my pastor as You have given him to be an encouragement to me. Amen.

Bargain with God?

BIBLE READING: *Psalm 47*

Ferdinand, who later sent Columbus on his voyage, was about to become king. But before he could receive his crown, he had to kneel before a judge. This

judge read a letter from the nobles that said: "We who are as good as you accept you as our king only if you accept all our privileges, liberties, and laws. But if you don't accept these, neither will we accept you as king."

This is the way many people accept God as king. They will accept Him only if He does what they want. They will worship and serve Him if He makes the sun shine on their picnic day. They will put money in the offering if He says yes to all their prayers. They will do some good deeds if He gets them a new bike. They will quit stealing if He keeps them from getting caught this time.

If we treat God this way, we are not really accepting Him as our king. We are treating Him as a servant with whom we can bargain.

When we have true faith, we accept God without any ifs, ands, or buts. We believe that He always does what is loving and wise. So we have no need to bargain with Him. If He doesn't always make things turn out the way we like, we believe it's because He has a better way.

How insulted the almighty God must be when we human beings try to bargain with Him! Yet He loves us and gave His Son to die for us. He only asks us to accept Him as our King and trust Him without question. In other words, He wants us to have faith in Him.

And why is He so anxious for us to accept Him? For our own good, because when we accept Him, we are accepting also the salvation He brings.

To think about: What bargains have you tried to make with God? Why is it foolish to bargain with God? Why is God so anxious to have you accept Him as King?

I need help, Lord. Teach me to trust You so I will serve You as my King. Amen.

Made Just Right

BIBLE READING: *Psalm 139:13-18*

Suppose you could have chosen where you would be born, also the kind of house and even the century. Would you have chosen a different place and time for your birth? Maybe so. But you didn't have that choice. After all, you're not God.

The strange thing is, God had a choice. And look what He chose for His Son—Bethlehem! And a stable!

Mark Twain once visited the Holy Land. He saw its barren hills and its dirty cities like Bethlehem. He asked, "If God wanted His Son to be born into this world, why didn't He pick some nice place like Lake Tahoe?" (Lake Tahoe is a beautiful mountain lake on the California-Nevada border and is now a famous resort.)

Of course God could have chosen such a birthplace for His Son. He could also have chosen our own century so Jesus could enjoy all our modern gadgets and easy living. But He didn't. He chose instead just the right time and place in which Jesus could best serve and save us. God chose what He did because that was the choice just right *for us.*

Maybe you weren't born at just the time and place you like best. And maybe you wish you were born with a better body—a taller or thinner one, one with a better-looking face or a smarter brain. Well, don't feel bad. God chose where and when you would be born, also the body you were born with. And what He chose for you is *just right* for you.

Everything God chooses for us is just right—like the time and place Jesus was born. True, someday we will live in a far better place and in a far better body. That will be when time turns to forever. Meantime we are living in the time and place and body that is just right for us right now. So let's enjoy what we have, make the best use of it, and thank God for it.

Heavenly Father, thank You for making me the way I am. The way You made me is just right for me. I believe this because I know You love me. Keep me from ever forgetting this. Amen.

Past the Parking Lot

BIBLE READING: *Luke 11:27-28*

Church was over, and the people had all gone home. A passerby who happened to be taking a shortcut through the church's parking lot found several Sunday school leaflets on the ground. By now they were wrinkled and dirty. On the cover of the leaflets he saw a picture of Jesus being taken down from the cross.

The man thought to himself, "Surely these lesson papers were meant to be taken home and read again and again. But some children cared so little about them that they just threw them away. I wonder if that's also what happens with what people hear and learn in church. Maybe it never gets past the parking lot."

Is this true? Just what do we do with what we hear in Sunday school and church? Do we keep what we have heard? Do we treasure God's Word in our heart and live it throughout the week? Or do we forget it by the time we reach the parking lot?

The Bible says about Jesus' mother: "Mary kept all these things, pondering them in her heart" (Luke 2:19). This is what God wants us to do with His Word. He wants us to keep it in our hearts and live it at home, at school, at the playground, and wherever we go.

God's Word gives us all the tremendous blessings Jesus has won for us. Let's not lose these blessings at the parking lot. Jesus said: "Blessed are those who hear the Word of God *and keep it!*"

To think about: What did you learn from God's Word the last time you went to Sunday school and church? In what way has what you learned become a part of your life since?

Almighty God, Thy Word is cast
Like seed into the ground;
Now let the dew of heaven descend
And righteous fruits abound. Amen.

Independence Celebration

BIBLE READING: *Matthew 26:26-28*

John had often seen his parents go to Holy Communion. But this particular Sunday, as he and his family were driving home from church, he got curious about it. "Dad," he asked, "what is Communion all about?"

"Well," his father answered after giving the matter some thought, "you might say it's our independence celebration."

"Independence? I thought we celebrate that on July Fourth."

"That," his father replied, "is the *United States'* Independence Day and is something quite different. People celebrate that Independence Day with fireworks displays. I guess the fireworks are to remind us of how the United States won its independence — by war and fighting.

"Communion is the *Christian's* independence celebration. We are really celebrating our freedom from sin and hell. And Communion reminds us how this independence was won. For when Jesus began this supper, He said, 'This is My body.' He also said, 'This is My blood of the covenant, which is poured out for many for the forgiveness of sins.'

"You see, we didn't do any fighting to win our independence from sin and hell. Jesus did all the fighting, the suffering, and the dying for us."

As John's father pointed out, Holy Communion reminds us of how Jesus won forgiveness for us. But, of course, His body and blood are more than just reminders of how we got freedom from sin and hell. They also give and guarantee that freedom. Before He died, Jesus made a solemn will, or promise, to forgive all our sins. In Communion He is signing and sealing that promise with His own blood.

No wonder God's people look forward to receiving this supper as often as they can!

To think about: Of what does Holy Communion remind us? Why do you look forward to going to the Lord's Supper often?

Lord, Thy holy body into death was given,
Life to win for us in heaven.
No greater love than this to Thee could bind us.
May this feast thereof remind us. Amen.

One for All

BIBLE READING: *Isaiah 53*

During World War II an angry Japanese officer paced up and down before a group of American prisoners on Corregidor Island. "One of you stole a can of food!" the officer roared. "Whoever did it, step forward and die like a man! Otherwise everyone of you will be punished."

The American officer who had stolen the food was afraid to come forward. After a long period of silence a small sailor stepped forward to take the blame and the consequences. He hoped in this way to save the other prisoners.

"You are a brave man," the Japanese officer said with a smile. And to everyone's surprise he rewarded the hungry sailor with a large can of corned beef.

When Jesus carried His cross out to Calvary, He was stepping forward to take the blame for our sins. And although He was innocent, He really had to suffer the consequences. For, as the Bible says, the Lord was laying on Him the iniquity of us all.

Jesus was put to death by crucifixion, one of the most horrible tortures ever invented. Why did Jesus volunteer for such punishment? Because He loved us so much that He was willing to sacrifice Himself for us — One for all.

But like the sailor, Jesus was rewarded for His heroic deed. The Father in heaven granted Him His heart's desire. This desire Jesus expressed in His prayer on the cross: "Father, forgive them" (Luke 23:34). Therefore Jesus could look down through all the ages of history and see that we and all other people have been forgiven because of His suffering. And so He died satisfied.

O Jesus blest, My Help and Rest,
With tears I now entreat Thee:
Make me love Thee to the last,
Till in heaven I greet Thee. Amen.

Take Heed How You Hear

BIBLE READING: *Psalm 85*

The famous missionary Samuel Zwemer was pleasantly surprised. He noticed that the people of Arabia eagerly read every bit of Christian literature he placed into their hands. But later he discovered that the people were paying no attention to what the literature said. They were only enjoying the beautiful Arabic in which it was written.

Though we receive the Word of God in many ways, we too can miss its message and the salvation it brings. We can enjoy the beautiful music of a hymn without even thinking about the hymn's message. We can turn our Sunday school lessons into mere interesting stories and challenging activities. We can make of our Bible reading and home devotions nothing but practice sessions in reading skills. Yes, it is possible for us to read and hear the Word of God day in and day out without receiving our Savior, who comes to us through that Word.

Jesus said of some people: "Seeing they do not see, and hearing they do not hear, nor do they understand" (Matthew 13:13). This is why Jesus not only told us to hear His Word but added: "Take heed then *how* you hear." (Luke 8:18)

Simply to have God's Word register on our eardrums is not enough. Neither is it enough to see His Word with our eyes. We need to see and hear it deep in

93

our hearts. But this kind of seeing and hearing only God can give us. This is why the psalmist prayed: "Show us Thy steadfast love, O Lord, and grant us Thy salvation. Let me hear what God the Lord will speak."

It's a good idea to pray such a prayer and to pray it daily. For with God's help we hear and learn the message of His love deep in our hearts. And by His help we get more out of His Word than just words. We receive our Lord Himself. And for us that means eternal life!

To do: Make up a prayer you might use before going to Sunday school and church or before you begin your home devotions.

Lord, open Thou my heart to hear,
And through Thy Word to me draw near;
Let me Thy Word e'er pure retain,
Let me Thy child and heir remain. Amen.

A Humorous Situation?

BIBLE READING: *Luke 6:41-42*

It sounds like a humorous situation in a movie cartoon. Imagine someone insisting on removing a speck in another person's eye while being so blind as not to notice a log hanging out of his own eye! Yet Jesus warns us that we may be guilty of just such stupidity.

Are we? We are if we condemn other people for their faults. For then we are being blind to our own faults.

In his poem "To a Louse," Robert Burns tells about a well-dressed woman sitting in church. She was dressed so grandly that she must have thought everyone was surely admiring her. But what people saw was a louse crawling up the back of her bonnet.

Burns wrote, "O that some Power the gift would give us to see ourselves as others see us." If we could see ourselves as God sees us, we would realize that the worst faults we see in others are mere specks compared with the faults God sees in us.

To go after the evils in other people in a fault-finding way is a dangerous game. For God can play that game too. And considering how many faults He can find in us, it is a most unsafe game for us to play.

What should we do then? First we should remove our own faults. "Then," Jesus says, "you will see clearly to take out the speck that is in your brother's eye."

But if we try to remove our faults, our sins, we quickly discover how impossible this is. God alone can remove them. And, thank God, He did. Instead of going faultfinding after us, He let men find fault with and condemn His faultless Son. Now He forgives all faults in us. And now we see clearly how to treat the faults in others: in the same way God has treated our faults — with mercy and forgiveness.

To think about: What faults do you have? How does God treat them? Is this the way you treat faults in others?

Lord, keep me from finding fault with others. Instead remind me that You have forgiven all my faults. And help me share this forgiveness with others. Amen.

What Price Peace?

BIBLE READING: *Luke 6:37-38*

With the help of a computer a man in Norway turned up these startling facts: Since man first began to keep written records, 185 generations of people have lived on the earth. But only 10 of these generations have lived without a war taking place somewhere on the face of the globe.

We may wonder, "Why must nations always make war on each other?" The answer, of course, is: "For the same reasons that we as individuals quarrel and fight with one another." And by searching our own lives, we can discover what these reasons are.

One reason for so many of our quarrels is our quickness to condemn and our slowness to forgive. How often we excuse our fights by saying, "But he hit me first"! And how many of our quarrels we could have nipped in the bud by a simple act of forgiveness! But we find it too tempting to get even first. And that's what really triggers things.

So often we are willing to forgive the other person only if he first apologizes. Surely this is not a fitting way for God's people to behave. God didn't wait for us to say we're sorry before He forgave us. Through Christ He turned away His anger from us even before we had a chance to be sorry for our sins. Shouldn't we, then, be willing to take the lead in forgiving others? Besides, if we refuse to forgive others, we set up a barrier between ourselves and God's forgiveness.

We may not be able to bring about peace between nations, but we can live at peace with those around us. The price for that peace is our readiness to forgive. But when we consider how much God forgives us, is it so large a price to pay?

To think about: What quarrel have you had lately? How does God want you to end such quarrels? Did you? What good reasons do you have for taking the lead in forgiving others?

O Lord, give me that peace which only Your forgiveness can give. And help me spread that peace by my forgiving others. Amen.

Knowledge for Help Power

BIBLE READING: *1 Timothy 4:11-16*

Knowledge isn't important?

While on an African safari a traveler discovered one morning that his landrover wouldn't start. And the nearest mechanic was more than 100 miles away! The traveler tried everything he knew, but nothing he tried would get the engine started. So he was forced to radio for the mechanic.

When the mechanic arrived, he took one look at the engine and tapped it twice with a wrench. The engine started immediately. "That will be one hundred dollars," said the mechanic.

"One hundred dollars just for two taps on the engine?" the traveler roared.

"No," answered the mechanic. "Ten cents for the taps and ninety-nine dollars and ninety cents for *knowing where* to tap."

Knowledge is important. Some people want knowledge because it brings them money. Others want knowledge because it brings them power over other people. Children of God want knowledge because it increases their ability to help people.

We who are God's children already have the most important knowledge in the world. We know Jesus. And by knowing Jesus we know God and His love, and we have the forgiveness, life, joy, and hope He gives. But just because we already have this most important knowledge doesn't mean we should ignore other knowledge. What we learn, even about geography, history, and science, may give us just what we need to help someone.

Of what use would your doctor be to you if he couldn't tell the difference between indigestion and appendicitis? We depend on the knowledge of our doctors. And how many people we haven't even met yet may some day depend on what we are learning right now! Let's not let them down. Let's learn everything we can so we can serve them well as our Lord wants us to.

To think about: What have you learned that has already given you the ability to help someone?

Lord Jesus, many of Your enemies are learning all they can so they can do great evil. Help me learn all I can, and give me Your Holy Spirit so I will use my knowledge to do good. Amen.

No Magic Formula

BIBLE READING: *John 14:12-14*

Is there some way we can make certain we will get what we pray for? Yes, said an ad in a national magazine. For only $1.49 you could get a book entitled *The Magic Formula for Successful Prayer*. The ad claimed that this book could show us a foolproof way of praying so we'd get the things we want, such as money, health, and influence over others.

Most Christians know better than to believe in such magic formulas. Yet we may think of Jesus' name as a magic prayer formula. For Jesus promised: "Whatever you ask in My name, I will do it." But He didn't mean that just tacking His name on the end of our

prayers would automatically get us whatever we pray for.

Perhaps this will help us understand what Jesus did mean: When Sergeant Shero told Private Craft to scrub the base chapel floor, he also told him, "If you need anything, just let me know. I'll see that you get it." But Sergeant Shero didn't mean such things as a private swimming pool or a trip around the world. He meant things like a bucket and scrub brush—things that Private Craft needed to carry out his assignment of scrubbing the chapel floor.

Jesus has given us an assignment—to spread the good news of His love by our words and deeds. When we ask for the things we really need *to carry out Jesus' assignment,* we are praying in Jesus' name. And these things He promises to give us.

That's not the same as using Jesus' name as a magic formula, is it? Wouldn't it be terrible if there were a magic formula to prayer? Then anyone could get whatever he wanted, no matter how selfish, wicked, or harmful it might be. But isn't it wonderful to know that Jesus will give us everything we really need to serve Him?

To think about: What do you really need to serve the Lord the way He wants?

Ask Jesus to give you these things you need to serve Him.

Why Bodies Wear Out

BIBLE READING: *Romans 8:18-25*

Mark's tooth ached a lot. But what bothered Mark most was that the dentist said the tooth must come out. And this was not a baby tooth but a permanent one. "Why didn't God give us bodies that never wear out?" Mark wondered.

Mark was beginning to discover something important about the world. Everything in it is "futile"— to use the word our Bible reading uses. This means that earthly things are like a wisp of smoke. One moment we see them, and the next they are gone.

We may think God has played a mean trick on us by making things wear out. But as long as we are still sinful it would not be good for us to have everything the way we want. If we did, we'd soon ignore the hope God has given us. We'd be like little children on Christmas morning who get so "wrapped up" in their presents that they don't want to take time out for church.

So God has things wear out—our bodies too. He allows sickness, pain, and loss to come our way. But all this is an act of mercy on His part. Through these things He makes us long for better things. He reminds us of our hope in Christ—of the day when everything will be perfect, nothing will wear out, and we will be forever with the Lord. And what God leads us to hope for is no mere wish. It is real. Because of what Jesus has done for us, St. Peter writes, it is already "reserved in heaven for you." (1 Peter 1:4 KJV)

God has made the world futile because He doesn't want us to lose this hope. So for now we will experience some suffering and sadness. But St. Paul wrote: "I consider that the sufferings of this present time are not worth comparing with the glory that is to be revealed in us." When that day comes, we will see how right Paul was.

To think about: What signs do you see that the world is futile? How do these things make you think about your hope? What hope has God given you?

Father, help me to enjoy and work for the world You've given us to live in. But keep me from losing sight of You and the life You have prepared for me through Christ, my Lord. Amen.

Thanks but No Thanks

BIBLE READING: *Ephesians 5:17-20*

She's crying. Her family doesn't hear her; they've all finished their supper and have left the table.

Still, God hears her because her crying is really a prayer. This is what she's praying:

"Forgive me, Lord. I thanked You before for this food. But I guess You heard what I really said in my heart. I'm sorry, Lord, but I can't help it. I just don't like the stuff!

"I know I'm wrong. I should like what You give me, but I have all these dislikes deep inside me. For milk and tomatoes and noodles. And for so many other things besides food—certain people and clothes, and rainy days and church even.

"O God, I'm sure Jesus wasn't this way. How come I am? I guess it's because I'm sinful. Forgive me, Lord, for Jesus' sake. And please do me a favor. Help me to like this stuff. I'll try it again if You'll help me.

"And help me to like everything You give me— clothes and people and just everything that's from You. They must be good for me if You send them, because You're good.

"And one thing more, Lord. If I must dislike some things, help me to dislike what You dislike. I mean things like selfishness and pouting and—well, You know, Lord.

"Now I'm going to quit praying and start eating. But please, Lord, don't go away. I'm really going to need Your help. Amen for now. Oh, and thanks. This time I mean it."

Her prayer makes you wonder, doesn't it? We usually think what we dislike is bad and what we like is good. But maybe the girl is right. Maybe our likes and dislikes are sometimes a bit mixed up.

To think about: Can you name some things God has given you that you dislike? Can you name some things God dislikes but you sometimes like?

Heavenly Father, forgive me for sometimes liking and disliking the wrong things. Make me more like Jesus. I know His "tastes" never got mixed up. In His name I pray. Amen.

The Do-Nothing Sin

BIBLE READING: *Luke 16:19-31*

In His parable of the rich man and Lazarus, Jesus does not picture the rich man as a criminal. He was not a murderer, a robber, or a child-beater. Yet when he died, he went to hell. Why?

A sickly beggar named Lazarus lay at the rich man's gate, where prowling dogs came and licked his sores. The rich man had not made Lazarus sick. Neither had he turned the dogs on Lazarus. What, then, had he done that was so bad?

It was not what he had done but what he had not done. He had done nothing to help poor Lazarus except perhaps allow him to eat some garbage. God had commanded: "You shall love your neighbor as yourself" (Leviticus 19:18). But the rich man was so busy enjoying himself—eating the best foods, wearing the finest clothes—that he just didn't bother to love Lazarus. That was his crime.

Some of the worst sins we commit are not the bad things we do but the good things we fail to do. Before the American Civil War, few people actually bought or sold slaves. But how many never so much as said a word against slavery! During World War II few people in Germany actually took part in the murder of 6 million Jews. But how many never lifted a finger to help the Jews! Few people deliberately lead people into unbelief. But how many do nothing to lead them out of it!

The Bible says, "Whoever does not do right is not of God, nor he who does not love his brother" (1 John 3:10). Though we may not be aware of it, we are committing terrible sins every day just by failing to love as we should. How much, then, we need God's forgiveness!

To think about: People are poor in many different ways. What are some of the ways? These poor may not be lying at your gate, but where are they? How can you help them? Do you always do so?

O God, I don't deserve Your love, because I have been so loveless. Forgive me for Jesus' sake. And by Your love for me, help me to be more loving toward the people who need my love. Amen.

Source of All Things
BIBLE READING: *1 Corinthians 8:6*

Michelangelo was a man of unusual artistic powers. One of his most famous works, a statue of Moses, looks so real that a person might almost expect to see the statue's lips form words. In fact, some say that when Michelangelo finished the statue he gave it a final blow with his mallet and said, "Now, speak!" With chisel and mallet Michelangelo could turn a block of marble into a work of art. But not he or anyone else could give it life.

Many people wonder, "Where, then, does life come from?"

Some people answer, "Life started all by itself." But an English scientist said that the chances of life starting up all by itself are 400,000 trillion trillion trillion trillion to one. Where, then, does life come from? The Bible says: from "God, the Father, from whom are all things." This is why we call God "Father." All things come from Him. He designed and made dead things like marble and living things like you.

Some things, though, are no longer the way God designed them. They have become evil and hurtful. God made all things good. But we by our sins have spoiled so much of God's handiwork. By our sins we have even ruined ourselves. Worst of all, we can no more unruin ourselves than Michelangelo could change a piece of marble into a living Moses.

But God our Father can help us and has helped us. Besides being the Source of all life, He is the Source of all mercy. In mercy He designed and carried out His great rescue operation. He sent His only Son to take away our sins. And through His Holy Spirit He adopted us into His family. Now He loves and cares for us more than any earthly father could ever hope to do.

So we have a double reason to call Jesus' Father "our Father." Aren't you glad that you can?

To think about: In what two ways is God your Father? How does knowing that the Creator and Controller of the universe is your Father give joy to your life?

God, You are my Father, the One to whom I can turn in every need. To You I turn now to give thanks for all Your gifts and mercy. Amen.

Agent of All Things

BIBLE READING: *Colossians 1:15-20*

For thousands of years people dreamed of a way to get through the Alps between France and Italy. A few passes do wind through the mountains, but these are closed much of the year by the long winter snows. And in these narrow passes many travelers and soldiers have plunged to their death.

In 1965, though, the dream at last came true. After years of labor an auto tunnel was cut right through Mont Blanc, one of Europe's highest mountains. Now through this tunnel people can travel safely and easily between France and Italy.

Sin is a barrier far more deadly and impassable than the Alps. It stands between us and God, between us and heaven. But our heavenly Father sent His Son into our world to be like a tunnel cut right through our sin barrier. So no matter how high our sins tower over us, God's forgiveness and love get through to us. For they come *through* Jesus.

It all seems so simple — now. But tunneling through the barrier of our sins cost Jesus years of toil and pain. Finally He had to suffer wounds and nails, cross and death. His Father did not spare Him from all this. For God the Father always uses His Son as His Agent *through* whom He does things. Through His Son He created the world. Through His Son He rules and preserves the world. Through His Son He will judge the world. And it was the Father's will that through His Son we should receive forgiveness and eternal life.

Some people are still cut off from God. But no one needs to be. Through Jesus we all have an open road right to the Father's loving heart. Do you believe in Jesus? If so, you're on the right road. You're going through Jesus to the Father. And through Jesus the Father comes to you.

To think about: In what ways is Jesus the heavenly Father's Agent? In what way do you need Jesus for your Agent?

O Jesus, through whom I come to the Father, I thank You for all that You suffered to bring me the Father's mercy. And bring me one day to Your Father's home above. Amen.

Completer of All Things

BIBLE READING: *Romans 11:36*

No doubt you've heard the expression "electrical circuit." A circuit describes something that travels in a circle or makes a round trip. Have you ever wondered why we use the word "circuit" in connection with electricity?

Some kinds of electricity do make round trips. Take a bicycle light. Electricity flows *from* the batteries along one wire, *through* the lightbulb, and then back *to* the batteries along a second wire. The bulb will not light up unless this circuit, or round trip, is complete.

St. Paul describes another kind of circuit when he writes: "*From* Him [God] and *through* Him and *to* Him are all things." If something does not follow this circuit, it is not really complete as God designed it to be. This includes also God's plan for our salvation.

We have come *from* God, for He made us. *Through* His Son God sends us all our blessings, including His forgiveness and love. And God says to us: "Return *to* Me with all your heart" (Joel 2:12). We return to God through faith in Jesus.

The trouble is, our sinful nature won't let us return to God. It wants to do exactly as it wishes and not as God wishes. If our sinful nature has its way, God's plan of salvation for us will be incomplete.

So God sends the Holy Spirit into our hearts. He overcomes our sinful nature and leads us to faith in Jesus. And this faith makes such a change in us that we find ourselves wanting to live with God and for God.

In this way the Holy Spirit is returning us to God. He is completing God's plan for our salvation. In fact, He is the Completer of all things. But His final act of returning us to God is yet to come. On the Last Day He will raise us from the dead so we can live with God forever.

To think about: What signs do you see in your life that the Holy Spirit has returned you to God?

O God of my salvation, fill me with Your Holy Spirit so my whole life will be one continuous hymn of praise and glory to You. Amen.

A Gun at Our Head?

BIBLE READING: *1 John 4:20-21*

In the movie *Dr. Zhivago* the hero gets quite a shock at his homecoming. He had been with the Russian army fighting against the Germans. But when he returned home, he found his large, beautiful house swarming with people from the slums.

Dr. Zhivago was about to ask what all these people were doing in his house. But a communist official spoke first.

"Shame on you," he scolded Dr. Zhivago, "living alone all these years in such a big house! There's enough room here for thirteen families. So we've moved some families from the overcrowded slums into your house." Dr. Zhivago had failed to share with the needy when he had a chance. Now he was being forced to share.

Scenes like this actually happened in Russia. They could happen here. The Bible warns: "He who gives to the poor will not want, but he who hides his eyes [from the poor] will get many a curse." (Proverbs 28:27)

Often it's so easy to hide our eyes from the poor. Maybe we can avoid going through those parts of town where the poor live. We can steer clear of a lonely old man who is always looking for someone to talk to. We can pretend we don't know about the youth down the street who is friendless. In fact, we can live content and carefree as if there were no one in the whole wide world who desperately needs our love and help.

Surely we Christians don't need the communists to hold a gun to our head before we'll share with the needy. Christ's cross has been held before our eyes. That is enough, isn't it? We can't see His love for us and then ignore those who need our love and help, can we?

To think about: What would your life be like without Jesus' love? What did it cost Jesus to help you? Who needs your help? What will you do to help those persons?

Loving Lord, turn my pretty words about love into powerful deeds of love. In Your name I pray. Amen.

Silly "Cures"

BIBLE READING: *Galatians 3:10-14*

You've heard of silly cures? How's this one:
Back in the year 1888 Jacksonville, Florida, was stricken by an epidemic of yellow fever. Almost 5,000 people caught the disease, of whom more than

400 died. At that time people didn't know they could stop the epidemic simply by getting rid of the mosquitoes that carry yellow fever.

In a vain effort to stop the epidemic, the army brought in artillery and tried to bombard the germs they thought were in the air. At the post office, workers spread on the floor all letters being mailed out of Jacksonville. Then, to kill the germs on the letters, they beat them with spiked clubs. These efforts did nothing to stop the epidemic, but they sure succeeded in hurting people's eardrums and in messing up the mail.

We may think, "How foolish for people to think they could get rid of germs with cannons and clubs!" Yet today there are many people who are even more foolish. They think they can get rid of their sins by doing good deeds.

Of course, God wants us to do good deeds because they are helpful to our neighbors. But when it comes to removing sin, our good deeds do no more good than those cannons and clubs did in getting rid of yellow fever.

Jesus' death on the cross is the only real cure for sin. And Jesus now invites us to make use of this cure. We do so by believing in Him. The Bible says: "Everyone who believes in Him receives forgiveness of sins." (Acts 10:43)

Since God has "put us wise" to the real cure for sin, let's teach other people about Jesus' cure. Our laughing at their own "cures" won't help them. But pointing them to Jesus will.

To think about: In what way are good deeds worthwhile? In what way are they useless? What is the

115

only real cure for sin? How do we make use of this cure? Are you doing so?

> I am trusting Thee, Lord Jesus,
> Trusting only Thee;
> Trusting Thee for full salvation,
> Great and free. Amen.

A Guiding Star

BIBLE READING: *Philippians 2:14-16*

Long ago God used a star to lead the Wise Men to the Christ Child. He still uses "stars" to lead people to Jesus. But the guiding "stars" He uses today are not shining heavenly bodies. They are ordinary people, like your parents, pastors, Sunday school teacher, and friends. Without such guiding stars in our life we might never have known our Savior or might have forgotten Him long ago.

The book *A Tale of Two Cities* tells how God used one man as a guiding star. His name was Sydney Carton. He had gone to visit a man who was in prison waiting to be executed. But Carton did more than just visit. He exchanged places with the man. So the real prisoner escaped, and Carton was led out to die in his place.

One of the other prisoners who was to be executed with him was a young woman. She recognized that Carton was not the man who had been sentenced to die with her. When she found out how Carton had traded places with his friend, she immediately thought of Jesus, who had traded places with all people. And in thinking about Jesus she lost her fear of dying.

The young lady said to Carton: "Except for you, I would not have been able to raise my thoughts to Him who was put to death that we might have hope and comfort here today. I think you were sent to me by heaven."

Wouldn't it be wonderful if our words and deeds would lead someone to Jesus? Wouldn't it be wonderful to hear someone say to us, "I think you were sent to me by heaven"? Well, we *have* been sent by heaven — to guide the people around us to Jesus. By our words and deeds at home, at school, and at play we can be one of God's 20th-century guiding stars.

To think about: Who are some of the guiding stars in your life? How have they helped lead you to Jesus? Can you recall a time you reminded someone of Jesus or led someone to Jesus?

Lord, I thank You for those who have brought me to You. Help me be a star guiding others to You. Amen.

Race with Death

BIBLE READING: *Luke 1:76-79*

For most people racing is fun. But sometimes a race can be a matter of life and death.

Such a race took place in 427 B. C. An army from Athens had put down a revolt on the island of Lesbos. Sometime afterwards the people of Athens voted to severely punish the rebel islanders. So they sent a ship full of soldiers to the island with orders to kill all the rebel men and to sell the women and children as slaves.

The next day the people of Athens were sorry they had sentenced the islanders to such terrible punishment. So they quickly sent a second ship with orders to pardon the rebels. But the first ship already had a full day's head start. The sailors on the second ship knew they were in a race with death. They had to catch the first ship before it was too late. Day and night they rowed, straining every muscle at the oars. Fortunately they caught up with the first ship and so saved the islanders.

Each day life-and-death races are going on all around us. Many people do not believe in Jesus. Others have never heard of His love and goodness. Each day these people are getting closer to the time of their death. When they die, it will be too late. They will have no further opportunity to believe in Jesus.

But our Savior has won pardon and eternal life for all. We who know this wonderful news must strain every muscle to bring the message to others. We can do this by our prayers, our offerings, and our witnessing to Jesus through word and deed. But we need to do it before it is too late. Remember, the race is a matter of life and death.

To think about: Even though a non-Christian friend is young, why isn't it wise to say, "I have plenty of time to tell him about Jesus"?

Lord Jesus, help me bring the message of Your love to others before it is too late. And may the Holy Spirit bless my telling of this good news. Amen.

People "Read" You

BIBLE READING: *2 Corinthians 3:1-3*

Long ago the Roman emperor Julian decided to persecute and destroy the Christian church. When someone asked him why he hated the Christian religion, he answered, "Never have I seen wild animals fight as viciously as Christians fight with one another."

Julian had been raised as a Christian, but the evil way some Christians treated one another had turned him against Christ and the Christian religion. Many people today also form their opinion of Jesus and

Christianity by the way they see Christians behave. If they see us treating people hatefully, they think there must be something wrong with our Lord and the religion we follow.

Of course, we know Jesus never taught us to hate anyone. He said: "This is My commandment, that you love one another as I have loved you" (John 15:12). It does not matter whether people are good or bad, whether they have hurt us or not, or whether they belong to the same race or religion to which we belong. Jesus wants us to love and be kind to everyone because He loves everyone and gave His life to save us all.

But many people don't know this. They have never read the Bible to see what Jesus really taught. They only "read" us. So they get their idea of Jesus by what they see us do.

Recently a missionary said: "When Christian people do and say evil things, this makes our work more difficult. But when the heathen see and hear how helpful Christians are and how kindly they treat people of other races and colors, our job of teaching the message of Jesus' love becomes much easier."

What do people read about Jesus in our lives? There's one fact we can't get around. Our lives do tell a story. But what story? The truth — that Jesus loves all and has saved all? Or a lie?

Father in heaven, forgive me for any lies my life has told about my Lord. Fill my heart with such love for others that my life may be a sermon preaching Jesus' love to the world. Amen.

Promise Keeper

BIBLE READING: *Matthew 1:18-25*

Would you keep a promise even if it meant your death?

Pythias said he would. Pythias was a man who lived long ago. He had angered the king and for this was sentenced to die. But he begged the king, "First let me journey to my homeland so I can tell my parents good-bye. I promise to be back by the day you've set for my execution."

"You'll never keep a promise like that," the king answered.

Pythias' friend Damon stepped forward and said, "If Pythias doesn't return, you can kill me instead." The king agreed although he was convinced that Pythias would never return.

When the day of the execution arrived, just as the king had suspected, Pythias had not returned. "Then let Damon die in his place," the king ordered.

They were about to kill Damon when they saw someone running toward them. It was Pythias. He apologized for being late but explained that he had been delayed by a shipwreck. The king's mouth dropped open. He was so amazed at Pythias' keeping his promise that he ordered him and his friend both released.

Well, to find someone who would keep such a promise is rare indeed. Think of all the much simpler promises we have broken. It's most unlikely, then, that we would keep a promise that would cost us our life.

Yet God did. Long ago He sent an angel to tell Joseph to name God's Son "Jesus," which means "Savior." Why this name? Because, said the angel, God's Son would "save His people from their sins." That was a promise—a promise that meant Jesus would have to keep an appointment with death on Calvary. And we know how He kept that promise.

As we face each new day, we do not know what evil may lie in wait for us. Yet we can live unafraid because God has promised to take good care of us. And we know He keeps His promises. The name "Jesus" is our constant reminder of this.

To think about: What did Jesus have to do to live up to what His name promises us? How does His keeping that promise help you to be unafraid in your everyday life?

Lord, when I am afraid, remind me of Your promise to care for me. Remind me also of how faithful You are in keeping Your promises. Amen.

Christ's Church for All

BIBLE READING: *Matthew 25:31-46*

While visiting England, the famous writer Erasmus was given a tour of a very beautiful church.

The ushers wanted to impress Erasmus with what a great honor they were showing him by allowing him to enter their church. They boasted, "We never let anyone in our church except the rich and people who are members of high society."

"Gentlemen," said Erasmus in his most biting tone, "I am indeed honored to be in a church where Christ Himself wouldn't be allowed!" And Erasmus was right. For Jesus was poor.

Some people want to exclude from their church and their love those who are not their kind of people. Even in Jesus' day some church people looked down their noses at certain people and resented Jesus' being a friend to them.

Jesus said that on Judgment Day He will accuse some people of having excluded Him from their help and love. They will be surprised at this and will ask, "When did we withhold our love and help from You?" He will answer: "Whatever you failed to do to the humblest of My brothers you failed to do to Me" (Phillips). So if we shut someone out of our church or heart, we are shutting Jesus out.

Jesus has included us among His friends. And He has made us members of His church. One way He now asks us to show our friendship for Him is by loving and befriending all His people. Whether they're rich or poor, good or bad, white or black, red or yellow, citizen or foreigner doesn't matter. Jesus has redeemed them all just as He has redeemed us. And He welcomes them into His church. Dare we do less?

To think about: Is there anyone you would not welcome to worship at your church? How do you know Jesus would want you to welcome everyone?

All are redeemed, both far and wide,
Since Thou, O Lord, for all hast died.
Oh, teach us, whatsoe'er betide,
To love them all in Thee! Amen.

No Empty Phrases

BIBLE READING: *Matthew 6:7-8*

Do you put your heart into your prayers?

The Buddhist people of Tibet don't believe it is really necessary to do so. They write their prayers on pieces of paper and put them in prayer wheels. Then they place the prayer wheels by a waterfall so the falling water will keep the wheels spinning. They do this because they think their gods will pay attention to what is written on the prayer slips so long as the prayer slips are moving. Once the people have their prayer wheels going, they go away and don't give their prayers another thought.

Jesus said that God doesn't hear such prayers. When a person's heart isn't in his prayers, they are nothing but vain, or empty, phrases.

Though we wouldn't think of putting our prayers in prayer wheels, we may easily become just as guilty of using empty phrases. We do this whenever we pray or "recite" prayers without thinking of what we're saying. This may happen when we say "grace" at meals, when we recite our bedtime prayers, and when we speak or sing our prayers at church.

When we pray, we are asking God to listen to us. But having "caught His ear," we insult Him if we proceed to think about other things instead of Him and of what we are saying to Him.

God wants to hear our prayers and grant our requests. This is why He has given us the privilege of calling on Him. Giving us this privilege cost Him the life of His own dear Son. But He paid that price so we sinners could again be on speaking terms with Him.

In prayer we have a privilege through which God showers us with blessings. So let's not waste this costly and wonderful privilege by using only "empty phrases."

To think about: How often do you usually pray each day? Are your prayers more than empty phrases? What might you do to make sure your heart is in your prayers when you pray?

O Thou by whom we come to God,
The Life, the Truth, the Way,
The path of prayer Thyself hast trod—
Lord, teach me how to pray. Amen.

Day of Joy

BIBLE READING: *Luke 21:25-28*

The day broke bright and clear on much of the world that first Sunday in December 1941. But for many people that day will always be remembered as a day of thick darkness. For on that day the Japanese delivered their surprise attack on Pearl Harbor.

One American seaman who watched the Japanese bombs and torpedoes send geysers of flame skyward exclaimed, "I didn't even know they were sore at us!" Yet he should have known. For some time American forces had been alerted that a Japanese attack was coming. The only questions were when and where.

For many people also the coming of Jesus to judgment will be a day of thick darkness. When the wicked hear their sentence, they may exclaim, "We didn't even know God was angry with us." But they should know. The Bible says: "God is angry with the wicked every day." (Psalm 7:11 KJV)

Yet God also says: "I have no pleasure in the death of the wicked but that the wicked turn from his way and live" (Ezekiel 33:11). God wants Jesus' coming to judgment to be a day of great joy for all people. This is why long ago God sent His Son into our world. Jesus' special assignment was to win our hearts back to God by the power of His loving sacrifice.

God wants no one to be surprised by Jesus' return to judgment. So God has made it unmistakably clear that Jesus *will* return. We do not know when, but that is unimportant. What is important is that we be ready. When we turn to God through faith in Jesus, we are ready. Then we can look forward to Jesus' return with great joy and hope, not with fear and trembling.

To think about: What has God done to make sure the Day of Judgment will not be a day of thick darkness for you? For whom else has He done this? Why do you look with joy for Jesus' return?

O my Savior, what a joy it will be to see You face to face and to live with You forever! Fill my whole life with this hope. And help me show this hope in the way I live with You also now in this world. Amen.

Where Jesus Is Born Today

BIBLE READING: *Luke 2:1-7*

Each Christmas season people from all over the world visit the Church of the Holy Nativity in Bethlehem. According to tradition, this church is built over the birthplace of Jesus.

Many visitors are surprised when they are shown the supposed place where Jesus was born. For it is not a stable but a grotto, or cave. Most Christmas cards, nativity scenes, and Christmas carols portray Christ's birthplace as a stable. Actually we can't be sure which it was. The Bible only tells us that Mary laid Him in a manger. So we know only that Jesus was born in a place usually reserved for animals.

Really, though, it doesn't matter where our Lord was born, whether in a stable or in a cave. What does matter is where He is born *today*. Jesus comes to us through His Word. And the place where He wants to be born today is in our hearts. Our hearts are no more worthy of heaven's King than was His first birthplace. Yet when Jesus is born in us, He transforms us into a holy shrine which the Father in heaven honors as the dwelling place of His dear Son.

Do you sense the honor? Jesus wants you for His birthplace. Do you see the glory? He brings you life that is forever. Can you possibly tell Him, "No"?

Redeemer, come! I open wide
My heart to Thee; here, Lord, abide!
Let me Thine inner presence feel,
Thy grace and love in me reveal;
Thy Holy Spirit guide me on
Until my glorious goal is won.
Eternal praise and fame
I offer to Thy name. Amen.

The Beaver's Birthday Party

BIBLE READING: *Luke 1:67-75*

There's a story about a beaver who invited all the animals round about to his birthday party. They all came but were soon so absorbed in the games and food that they paid no attention to the beaver. In fact, they crowded the poor fellow right out of his own house and locked the door.

The beaver sat outside alone and sad while inside everyone was having so much fun celebrating his birthday. All of a sudden the nearby dam began to break. This was no real danger to the beaver since he was an excellent swimmer. But what about the other animals inside his house?

Without giving it another thought, the beaver hurried to the dam and repaired the break, and just in time to prevent a flood. Only when the other animals discovered that he had saved their lives did they let him back into his own party.

Christmas is the day we celebrate Jesus' birthday. It has become the biggest party in the world. Yet like the selfish animals in the story, we may become so busy enjoying the celebration that we crowd Jesus right out of our Christmas. As we decorate trees, do Christmas shopping, exchange presents, and have family get-togethers, we may forget to honor Him whose birthday we are celebrating.

In the story the animals finally honored the beaver when they learned that he had saved their lives. What about us? Jesus was born to save us from eternal death and separation from God. Will we honor Him on His birthday? Will we give Him the center of our attention?

Not only on Your birthday, Lord, but every day lead me to honor You. For every day that I live I live only because of what You have done for me. Accept my praise, O Jesus, for Your saving love. Amen.

Bridge of Peace

BIBLE READING: *Isaiah 9:6-7*

Near Buffalo, N. Y., where only the Niagara River separates the United States from Canada, old cannons on both sides of the river are positioned to fire at the opposite shore. These cannons are no longer manned by soldiers. They are merely relics of the time over 150 years ago when the United States and Canada were at war with each other.

Today only a short distance from these cannons the International Peace Bridge spans the Niagara River, linking these two countries together. The name of the bridge is a constant reminder of the peace that now exists between the U. S. and Canada.

The sins we Christians commit each day are relics left over from the time when we were at war with God. God could interpret them as a renewal of the war on our part. In fact our sins *are* acts of war against God. So He would have every right to declare war on us. If He did, we know who would win the war. With His tremendous power He could destroy us in one blinding flash.

But because He is a God of love, He is always determined to bring peace between Himself and us. That's why He sent His own Son Jesus into our world. Jesus is the Bridge by which God has linked Himself with us in a bond of peace.

131

Through Jesus' birth on that Christmas Day long ago, God joined the human race. He took on our flesh and blood so that we might always be in His heart and mind. In Jesus' birth God declared "peace on earth, goodwill toward men."

So what shall we do? Go on with our warlike acts? No, let's celebrate the peace by giving glory to God in the highest.

To think about: What does the Peace Bridge link together? What does Jesus link together in a bond of peace? Some nations have used periods of peace to prepare for new wars. Is this the way you use the peace God has given you? How are you using this peace?

Dear Lord, fill my heart with joy in the birth of Your Son. Because You have sent Him to make peace between Yourself and me, keep me from all the warlike deeds of sin, for His sake. Amen.

Worse than Worthless

BIBLE READING: *James 1:22-27*

Jesus said: "He who is of God hears the words of God" (John 8:47). But what if a person hears the Word of God and does not live it? St. James writes that such religion is "vain," empty, worthless.

In fact it is worse than worthless. Such empty religion hinders the message of the Gospel. Charles Lee, an American general during the Revolutionary War, stated in his will that he did not want to be buried in any church or church cemetery. He said, "I have had so much bad company when living that I do not choose to continue it when dead." Imagine not wanting even to be buried near church people or a church!

Lee could think of church people as only "bad company." Why? Could it be that he had met too many churchgoers of the "hearing" but not the "doing" kind? Few things cause people to reject Christ's Gospel so fast as church people who are hearers only. If people usually hear us using our lips to curse, lie, and gossip, imagine how ugly the Gospel must sound to them coming from our lips! People can hear about the power of God's love. But won't it sound very weak to them if they see us, God's children, always quarreling at home and seldom being helpful to our neighbors?

It's easy to hear God's Word. Almost anyone can do that. But to believe it, to live it, that is another matter. It's not that we don't understand what God's Word says. It's that our old sinful nature simply wants to go on being sinful instead of adopting the way of faith and love.

Jesus has rescued us from our sins. But He also wants to rescue us from our sinful selves. So He gives us the Holy Spirit to turn our hearing of God's Word into God-pleasing doing. We are not helpless, then, no matter how strong our sinful nature is. With the Spirit's do-power we can rise above the sort of religion that is worthless and even worse.

O Spirit of God, fill me with faith in my Savior. For only then can my words and deeds help show Your love to the people around me. Amen.

Betrayer Betrayed

BIBLE READING: *Galatians 6:7-8*

His code name was "Cicero." During World War II he stole many top secrets from the British ambassador for whom he worked. He then sold these secrets to the Germans for more than a million dollars.

Some time later, when he tried to spend the money in South America, he was arrested for passing counterfeit bills. Cicero had betrayed the British but now found himself betrayed. For the million dollars the Germans had paid him was all counterfeit. This reminds us of what the Bible says: "Do not be deceived; God is not mocked, for whatever a man sows, that he will also reap."

What do you suppose would happen to us if God made us reap what we have sown? What if He treated us the way we have treated others or treated Him? Certainly He would be within His rights if He would get even with us by punishing us.

Yet the Lord Jesus came into this world to keep us from reaping what we have sown. He was betrayed by His friends, mistreated by His enemies, and finally put to death. He was reaping not what He had sown but what we have sown, so that we might never have to suffer what we deserve.

Now we can reap what Jesus has sown. We can be credited with all the kindness and love He showed, and we can receive the gift of heaven.

How can we reap all this? By believing in Jesus. As we live our faith in Him, we are "sowing to the Spirit." And from the Spirit, the Bible promises, we shall "reap eternal life."

To think about: In what way did Cicero reap what he had sown? Do you reap all the punishment you deserve? Why won't you ever have to? How are you showing Jesus your thanks for His reaping what you have sown?

Dear Lord, help me put my faith in You so I might reap what You have sown and not the evil I have sown. And help me show by my life that I appreciate all You have done for me. Amen.

Don't Laugh

BIBLE READING: *1 Corinthians 12:4-11*

This girl is learning an important lesson. She's trying to hit that little ball with that skinny bat. Whoof! Missed again! She couldn't hit a watermelon with a tennis racket.

She likes playing ball. It's good exercise. But she doesn't like being laughed at just because she isn't good at it. The boys make fun of her, but she knows they wouldn't like it if she *did* play as well as they do. What a world if everyone played ball as well as everyone else! Then no one could shine at it.

Besides, those boys would look pretty silly if they tried to play her violin. Maybe God never gave her the ability to be a ballplayer, but He surely blessed her with musical talent.

And there's the lesson: You don't have to be good at everything. In fact you can't be. God made us all different. He made some people good at playing ball. Others He made good at playing the violin. Still others He made good at arithmetic. Some people He made good at a number of things. But He made no one good at everything.

That's why we need one another. If we want to enjoy good music, some of us will always need people like this girl to play music for us. If we want to watch a good ballgame, some of us will always need players like those boys to play the game. And we all need

Jesus and His forgiveness. We need His forgiveness for the times we've laughed at others who don't have the same abilities we do. For we were really laughing at God. After all it is God who made them the way they are.

To think about: What's wrong with laughing at a person's clumsiness? What abilities do others have that God didn't give you? What abilities did He give you? How are you using them to serve others?

Lord, help me do my best with the abilities You've given me. And keep me from laughing at the way You've made others. Amen.

God's Clearest "Word"

BIBLE READING: *John 1:14-18*

Was David Livingstone dead? The outside world didn't know. People knew only that it had been quite some time since Livingstone had gone deep into unexplored regions of Africa to preach the Gospel.

A search party set out to find him. But since the searchers didn't understand the native languages, they were forced to question the people they met in a homemade sign language.

In one village the natives tried to tell the searchers that Livingstone had indeed been there and had given them cooking kettles. But misunderstanding the hand sign for "kettles," the search party reported to the government that Livingstone was arming the natives with cannons.

Misunderstandings like this happen every day. Many people try to figure out what God is like from the signs they see all around them. Because they see floods and tornadoes, wars and diseases, they think God is very cruel. Others think He doesn't care what happens to us.

To clear up such misunderstandings, God has sent us a message so clear that everyone should be able to grasp it. He sent His own Son into the world in human form so people could see, touch, and hear God for themselves. In everything Jesus did or said, He was showing us exactly how God feels about us. This is one reason the Bible calls Jesus "the Word" of God.

Through Jesus God has given us an unmistakable sign of His love for all people. Though wars and diseases, floods and tornadoes still occur we don't let such signs mislead us. For Jesus' sacrifice on the cross is God's clearest message to us. It tells us God loves us and is out to save us.

To think about: Suppose you were to get crippled in an accident. Would this lead you to doubt God's love for you? How does Jesus show that no matter what God allows to happen He still loves you?

Thank You, Father, for sending Your only Son to be such a clear message of how You really feel about me. Amen.

Captain Rogge's Answer
BIBLE READING: *Matthew 5:43-48*

Mrs. Green hung up the phone and turned to her son. "That was Mark Drew's mother," she said. "I guess you know what she called about. She said you started a fight with Mark."

"But sometimes he starts fights with me," Jim protested. "How else can I treat the guy? He's my worst enemy."

Like Jim, some people's only answer to hate is more hate. Is this the way we deal with our enemies? There is another way.

During World War II Bernhard Rogge, captain of the German warship *Atlantis,* sank or captured 22 American, British, and other Allied ships. From these ships he took aboard more than 1,000 people as prisoners of war.

We might suppose he would hate these prisoners. After all, they were his enemies and would probably kill him if they had the chance. Yet Captain Rogge treated them with kindness and love. He insisted on giving them as much food as he gave his own men. He also allowed them to swim in the ship's pool and from time to time gave parties for them.

Captain Rogge learned this way of dealing with enemies from Jesus, who said, "Love your enemies." This is God's own way. Though we were once God's enemies because of our sins, He returned only love as

He sent His Son to be our Savior. By doing this He has turned us from enemies into friends. Now he asks us, His friends, to be kind and forgiving to our enemies. Who knows but that in this way we may win their friendship?

By the way, after the war many of Captain Rogge's former prisoners sent him thank-you letters and CARE packages. His kindness had turned these enemies into friends. With God's help we may be able to do the same with our enemies.

To think about: How has God won your friendship? Do you try to win the friendship of your enemies by loving them? Suppose they keep on hating you even after you've shown them love. Should you then stop loving them? Why not?

Lord, teach me to treat my enemies not as they treat me but as You have treated me. Amen.

The Enemy Within

BIBLE READING: *Matthew 15:10-20*

A long time ago the people of Athens built a high wall around their city to protect themselves against the enemy Spartans. With thousands of soldiers stationed along the wall, the Athenians felt quite safe.

But there was another enemy right inside the city, an enemy so small that the Athenians hadn't noticed its presence. It was the germ that caused the plague, a deadly and highly contagious disease. Soon the Athenians were dying from the plague by the tens of thousands. Athens remained safe against the enemy outside the wall but was helpless against the enemy raging within.

One of the greatest dangers to us Christians is right inside us. Of course there are outside dangers to our faith, such as bad friends and filthy literature. Yet it does us no good to protect ourselves from such outside dangers if we fail to do something about the enemy that lurks inside us.

This enemy is our sinful nature, which hates God and His commandments. It may tempt us to fight, lie, cheat, and steal. Above all, it tries to kill our faith in Jesus.

Jesus has already taken the first step to destroy our inner enemy. When we were baptized, He gave us His Holy Spirit to war against our sinful nature. As we read and hear God's Word, we permit the Holy Spirit to continue the battle against our evil self. And the Spirit forms a new self in us, which is really Christ living in us.

142

Our sinful hearts still succeed in leading us into sin. But we can be thankful that the Spirit also brings us Christ's forgiveness. And because our victorious Lord lives in us, we can be sure that the final victory will be ours. St. Paul put it this way: "Who on earth can set me free from the clutches of my own sinful nature? I thank God there *is* a way out through Jesus Christ, our Lord." (Romans 7:24-25 Phillips)

To think about: In what way are you your own worst enemy? What has Jesus done to help you against your sinful self? What can you do to help the Holy Spirit war against your sinful self?

Holy Spirit, guard me every day against the sins without and within. And though I be plagued by them, still grant me the victory through my Lord Jesus Christ. Amen.

Your Voice for God

BIBLE READING: *Hebrews 10:22-25*

On May 16, 1860, the Republican party met in Chicago to elect a candidate for President of the United States.

Most people thought Senator Seward of New York would be elected. To make sure, his campaign manager brought a large cheering section to the convention. They were to persuade people to vote for Seward by cheering every time his name was mentioned.

Abraham Lincoln was not nearly so well known as Seward. But Lincoln's campaign manager found a man who was said to have leather lungs that could make more noise than Lake Michigan on a stormy day. This man along with many others formed a cheering section for Lincoln.

When the day for voting arrived, Lincoln's cheering section took up almost all the seats in the convention hall. Most of Seward's cheering section arrived too late to get in. So there was little cheering when Seward's name was mentioned. But when someone mentioned Lincoln's name, deafening cheers shook the building to its rafters. Many people were now convinced that Lincoln must be the most popular candidate. So they voted for him, and he won.

How would you like to use your voice for God as those people used theirs for Lincoln? Everywhere in the world there are plenty of voices to cheer for the devil. When people praise wicked deeds, they are cheering for the devil. Goods in a store window that tempt us to love them more than God are "voices" cheering for the devil.

In our church worship we have a special opportunity to cheer for God. We may not have leather lungs, but by our singing hymns and songs of praise we help persuade one another that Jesus is our best Friend and only Savior. In this way we "stir up" one another to love Him more. Then we are ready to go out into the world and "vote" for Jesus in all we do. Who knows how many others also we may persuade in this way to start voting for Jesus!

Lord, thank You for the voices of those who stir up my love for You. Help me use my voice to stir up their love also. Amen.

Visitor from Outer Space

BIBLE READING: *Psalm 8*

Many people believe UFOs (unidentified flying objects) are spaceships from another world. But one scientist told why he thought this was impossible:

"Maybe there are people living on some other world," he said. "And maybe these people are a thousand times more intelligent than we are. But space is so big they wouldn't know where to begin looking for us. Even if they detected radioactivity from our A-bombs or picked up our radar signals, our universe is so big it would take their spaceships many thousands of years to get here."

Isn't it a wonder, then, that God knows about us? Our earth is so small that if there were people living on some planet in our nearest neighboring galaxy they wouldn't be able to see our earth even with the world's largest telescope. Yet God sees our earth. He also sees every person on it. He sees even into our hearts — so great is His intelligence!

One would think the evil He sees in us would make Him want to forget all about us. But He doesn't. Instead He sent His Son "through space" to become one of us — a tiny speck on our tiny planet.

A psalmist wrote: "When I look at Thy heavens, the work of Thy fingers, the moon and the stars which Thou hast established, what is man that Thou art mindful of him, and the son of man that Thou dost care for him? Yet Thou hast made him little less than God and dost crown him with glory and honor."

Here is the greatest honor with which God has crowned us: He sent His Son to become one of us so that He might live and die for us. Now God's love is wrapped up in our world and us because His Son died for our world and us. So however big the universe, we know God's love can never lose track of us.

To think about: In what way is God's love for us even more amazing than His vast intelligence and power?

How great is Your goodness, O God! What a wonder that You can know us! And a greater wonder that You care for us! You came to live with us that someday we may live with You. Thanks be to You, my God, forever and ever. Amen.

Time's No Cure

BIBLE READING: *1 Timothy 6:11-12*

Some people think time will take care of everything. Apparently General Braxton Bragg was such
a person.

Standing on top of Missionary Ridge, he was
very pleased. His Confederate army had driven the
Union soldiers back into Chattanooga. And it now held
the whole horseshoe-shaped ring of mountains that
looked down on the sleepy Tennessee town.

Because their supplies had been cut off, the Union
soldiers in Chattanooga were going hungry. Their
horses and mules were starving. "In only a matter of
time," General Bragg announced, "the Union army will
have to surrender."

Some of his officers weren't so sure. "We can't
just sit here and wait," they advised. "We will have to
attack them to defeat them."

General Bragg refused. He was so sure that time
was on his side that he wrote Jefferson Davis, "I will
give you this Union army as a Christmas present." But
while he waited, the Union army found a way to get
supplies and reinforcements into Chattanooga. Finally
it grew so strong that General Grant gave the order
to attack.

Union soldiers went storming up Lookout Mountain and Missionary Ridge and drove the Confederate
army away in defeat. The army General Bragg thought

would be defeated by time turned around to defeat his own army.

How often do we say, "Time will take care of things"? We may feel our sinful habits will just die out in time — as we get older. But it doesn't work that way. We may feel in time we'll change into good students, or in time hatred between people of different colors will die out by itself without our having to battle against such hate.

Time is no cure for sin. Only Jesus is. So let's put no trust in time to change what is evil in us or in the world. Rather let's put our trust in Jesus. Then we receive His forgiveness and His power to fight and overcome evil. This, not time, is the cure for sin.

Lord Jesus, help me not to sit idle. With Your Spirit's power help me fight against every evil, and give me Your victory. Amen.

Exposed by a Camera

BIBLE READING: *2 Timothy 3:14-17*

During World War II John Larson was stationed in India. There he saw for himself some of the strange tricks of the fakirs. One fakir made a large rope stand in the air as straight as a board. A boy then climbed the rope higher and higher until he disappeared from sight.

John went back the next day to see the rope trick again. This time he took his camera so he could take pictures of the trick to send his family. He shot a number of pictures of the boy climbing the rope.

Later, when John examined the developed pictures, he was completely mystified. The photos showed clouds and empty sky but no boy climbing a rope — in fact no rope. After a while it dawned on John what had happened. He had been hypnotized. He had been tricked into thinking he saw the rope and the boy. But the camera revealed what he had really seen — empty sky.

John isn't the only one who can be tricked so easily. The devil can easily trick us into believing what is false. How often, for example, he tricks us into thinking that doing wrong will bring us real happiness!

Like John's camera, God's Word shows us the truth. It exposes such empty promises of the devil for what they really are — nothing but lies!

When it comes to knowing what is really good for us or when it comes to knowing God or even ourselves, we dare not trust our own eyes or minds or hearts. They're too easily fooled. What God's Word tells us, that we can trust. For it shows us the truth. And the greatest truth God's Word reveals to us is this: "Christ Jesus came into the world to save sinners" like us. (1 Timothy 1:15)

So the devil fools us from time to time. We are not being fooled when we believe that Jesus has saved even fools like us. God's Word says so.

To think about: Suppose something happens that makes it seem as if God doesn't love you. How can you find out whether or not He really loves you? Why can't you trust your own brain to figure out the answer?

Lord, by Your Word expose the lies of the devil. And let the truth of Your Word always speak right to my heart. Amen.

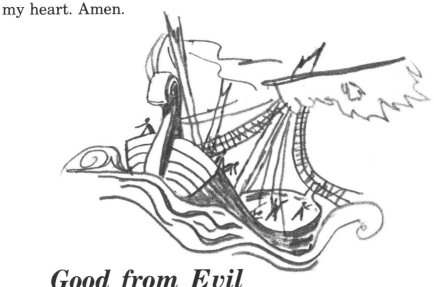

Good from Evil

BIBLE READING: *Acts 28:1-10*

The winter storms were already starting. St. Paul warned the captain against setting out to sea. But the captain insisted on sailing to a better harbor nearby.

The ship had barely left port when the storm struck. Giant waves hurled the ship like a straw before the wind. For 14 days the storm raged, driving the ship farther and farther off course. The people aboard gave up all hope of being saved. Yet God had other plans. On the morning of the 15th day the ship ran aground and was broken to pieces by the surf. But by clinging to broken planks Paul and all the others reached shore safely. The island on which they were shipwrecked was Malta.

St. Paul had always wanted to make a missionary trip to Rome. Getting shipwrecked on Malta along the way had not been part of his plans. Perhaps he wondered why God let this happen to him.

God used the shipwreck to give Paul an opportunity to do mission work on Malta. During the three months he was there Paul found many chances to witness for Christ and so bring the Christian faith to that island.

We can't always know why God allows evil things to happen to us. Often, though, He turns them into opportunities for us to serve Him in a new and better way. God puts some people in a hospital so they can be missionaries to other people in the hospital. He puts some people in a sickbed so they'll have more time for Bible reading and prayer.

Of this we can be sure: God turns every evil happening to our advantage. The Bible promises: "In everything God works for good with those who love Him" (Romans 8:28). After sending His Son to die for us, God certainly will not allow evil to harm us. He allows misfortune to come our way only because He always has a way of making it turn out good.

Heavenly Father, keep me from complaining when misfortune strikes. Help me see Your love at work even then. And give me opportunities for service even then. Amen.

Life-Saving Ambulance

BIBLE READING: *2 Corinthians 5:10*

The ambulance screamed down the street. At the hospital the heart-attack victim was rushed to the emergency room. But by that time he was already dead.

Scientists have invented equipment that can save many a victim of heart attack. Most hospitals now have this equipment. But by the time the patients get to the hospital, it is often too late. More than half the people who die from heart attack die within an hour after the attack begins. "How can we get them to the hospital faster?" many doctors have wondered.

At the Royal Victoria Hospital in Belfast, Northern Ireland, doctors found a solution. It took too long to bring the patient to where the life-saving equipment was. So they put the equipment in the ambulance. Now a patient can be treated *before* he reaches the hospital. In this way many lives are saved each year.

Jesus is like that life-saving ambulance. He rushes God's help to us before it is too late. At the Last Day we will all appear before the judgment seat of God. Many people are content to wait till then before doing anything about their sins. But *then* will be too late!

God knows we need treatment for sin *before* we stand in the Judgment. So He rushed Jesus to our rescue. To bring us God's cure cost Jesus His life. But by His life and death He saved us from dying forever.

153

So let God's judgment come. We know we shall stand before God cured of all sin, thanks to Jesus.

To think about: In what way is Jesus like the life-saving ambulance? How does Jesus give you confidence to face the Judgment?

Lord, when before Thy throne I stand
And cry aloud to Thee,
Then with the saints at Thy right hand,
Oh, grant a place to me. Amen.

Return to the Ages

BIBLE READING: *Acts 1:9-12*

It was just an ordinary Thursday. Peter, the other apostles, and Jesus were walking up the slopes of Mount Olivet. As they climbed, perhaps Peter was musing over some of the special things it seemed Jesus always did on mountaintops.

On a mountaintop Jesus preached His great Sermon on the Mount. On a mountaintop He called the Twelve to be His apostles. On a mountaintop He met with two visitors from heaven: Moses and Elijah. On a mountaintop He died for the sins of the world. On a mountain in Galilee the resurrected Jesus gathered His followers and promised them: "Lo, I am with you always, to the close of the age." (Matthew 28:20)

Though Peter may not have realized it at the moment, the Mount of Olives was about to become the Mount of Ascension. As the little band reached the top, Jesus turned and blessed them. Suddenly He began to rise into the air—higher and higher until He disappeared beyond the clouds. Our Lord had returned to heaven.

After the disciples recovered from their amazement, they realized that Jesus had also returned to the ages. For a few years in time the Son of God as a man had lived in an earthly town—first Bethlehem, then Nazareth, then Capernaum. Now He had gone to fill all things. He lives *everywhere*. Now Peter could walk the dusty trails of Palestine, John cross the ocean, and Thomas head across the desert. But Jesus would go with each of them, with all of them, wherever they went.

Jesus had left the first century to live in all the centuries. He continued to live in the first century with His disciples but also in later centuries with the crusaders, with the pilgrims, and in this age of astronauts also with us. Not time or distance or anything else can separate us from His presence or His power and love. No wonder the disciples returned from the mount rejoicing!

To think about: When Jesus returned to heaven, to what else did He return? Why does this make you glad?

We praise You, O Jesus, for Your glorious ascension. Someday take us with You to Your eternal home. Meantime help us find joy in knowing You are still with us. Amen.

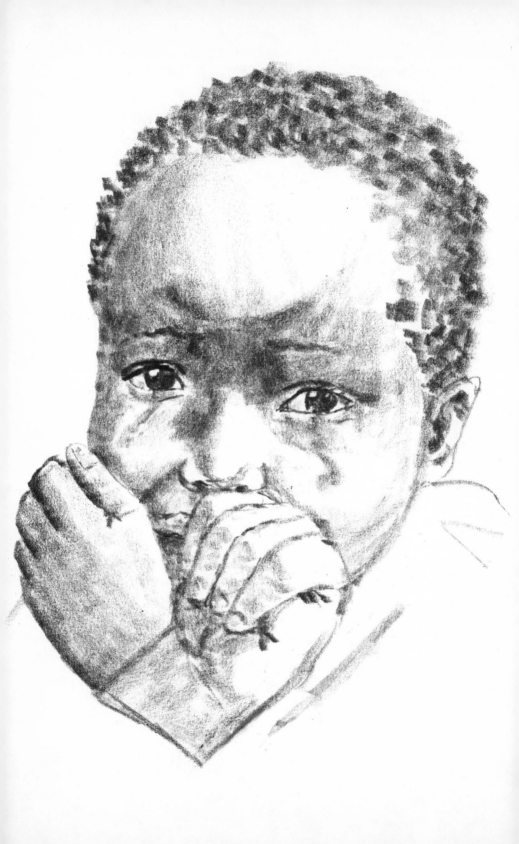

Gladdening Those with Tears

BIBLE READING: *Luke 24:45-53*

Some cry because they're lonely,
Some cry because they're mad,
Some cry because they're homely,
Most cry because they're sad.

The world's so full of sadness
I sometimes wish I might
Escape to heaven, where gladness
Shall always greet our sight.

But I'd forsake behind me
The poor, those full of fears;
To flee would be unkindly
While cheeks are stained with tears.

That's why God has me stay here—
To do as Christ above:
To wipe away each sad tear
By words and acts of love.

I can't yet leave for heaven,
Perhaps for many years,
So here I'll make a heaven
By gladdening those with tears.

To think about: According to the Bible reading, why didn't Jesus take His disciples to heaven with Him? How does the work He left them to do gladden those with tears? How can you share in this work? What other things can you do to bring gladness into someone's life?

Lord Jesus, help me spread kindness and love everywhere as You did. Then this earth will be a little more like heaven. Amen.

My Playground Your Roof

BIBLE READING: *Romans 15:1-3*

One of the interesting exhibits at Expo 67 in Montreal, Canada, was the Habitat. The Habitat was a series of apartment houses built in a very unusual fashion. Each apartment was so arranged that its roof served also as a neighbor's backyard. Such an arrangement allows each family in a crowded apartment building to have its own playground and garden. The Habitat has become a real experiment in cooperation. If you lived there, your roof would give someone else a play area, and your play area would give someone else a roof.

We can have such cooperation, though, even without living in the Habitat. We can use our play and recreation to refresh ourselves so we can serve other people better. And we can work hard so other people can have time for recreation.

Do you pitch in to help your mother with housework so she too can have free time? If you do, it's as if you make your roof her playground. Do you play to refresh yourself so you can do harder and better work? If so, it's as if you make your playground someone else's roof.

This is the way God wants us to cooperate with one another. Jesus Himself is our best example of such cooperation. Can you imagine Him playing just for His own fun? Or working just to serve Himself? No, all He did was also for others — for us and our salvation.

Through St. Paul God tells us: "Let each of you look not only to his own interests but also to the interests of others." (Philippians 2:4)

To think about: How can you have your play and relaxation serve the interests of others? For whom can your work provide relaxation? How?

Lord, help me think of others in all I do in work or play. Amen.

Too Late

BIBLE READING: *2 Corinthians 6:1-2*

On June 17, 1775, General Thomas Gage sent his British Redcoats forward to push the Americans off Breed's Hill. Thus began what is mistakenly called "the Battle of Bunker Hill." The British finally captured the hill on the third attack, but almost half their soldiers were killed or wounded. Even worse for the British, they could have captured the hill without firing a shot.

For a whole month before the battle General Gage knew he must keep the Americans off Breed's Hill if he were to protect Boston. He needed only to order his soldiers to occupy the hill, for the Americans had not yet arrived. But he waited and waited. By the time he finally did send his soldiers to garrison the hill, the Americans had already occupied and fortified it. It was too late to take the hill without a ruinous battle.

"Too late" could also be the story of our lives. If we always talk about what we plan to do in the *future* while we waste the time we have *now,* the future may well be too late. Next week or next year may be too late to begin the battle against sinful habits, to begin praying and a serious study of God's Word, to start being kind and helpful.

We do not know how much time we have left on earth to carry out the purpose for which God has made and redeemed us. The Bible tells us: "Now is the time of accepting. Now is the day of salvation."

Because Jesus has rescued us from our sins, we are living in the time of God's favor. But the time of His favor is right now. It is now Jesus invites us to put our trust in Him. It is now He says to us: "Follow Me."

Even tomorrow may be too late. So let's never put off to the future what our gracious God calls us to do today.

To think about: Is there something God has called on you to do that you have been putting off? Why is the "now" time always the best time?

Lord Jesus, be with me every day, and help me follow You every day till the end of days. Amen.

Least Likely to Succeed

BIBLE READING: *John 1:43-46*

Today Nazareth is a city of more than 40,000 people. It has grown a lot since the days when Jesus was a boy. Its white, sunbaked houses that once nestled on the side of a single hill now spill down into the plain and up over the surrounding hills.

Some things in Nazareth, though, haven't changed at all in the last 2,000 years. Along its narrow streets one can still see a carpenter shop that looks just like carpenter shops looked when Jesus lived there. On the white plaster wall hang several homemade saws. A single shelf holds assorted hammers, chisels, and box planes. Beneath the woodworking bench the floor is covered with shavings and scraps of wood. In our mind we can almost see the teen-age Jesus in the shop fitting legs on a table for one of His customers.

What did the people of Nazareth long ago think of this young carpenter? Perhaps some of them thought:

"Too bad about that boy. He's a careful worker and most polite, with a good head on His shoulders. But He'll never amount to anything. What with His father dead and His mother to support, He'll never be able to get a good education. Sure, He studies hard at the synagog school and once in a while goes to Jerusalem to learn from some famous rabbi. And He often studies late at night. But you need money and better schooling than that to get ahead in this world. Besides, He's a dreamer — going off alone into the hills to think and pray. No, of all the youths in this town, He's least likely to succeed."

But Jesus did succeed far beyond what anybody in Nazareth ever dreamed. He may not have had the shining opportunities some people have. But He made the most of the ones He did have. And with His Father's help He went out to change and save the world.

If you think you can never amount to anything, remember Jesus. With Him at your side you can do great things for God.

To think about: What opportunities do you have that Jesus didn't have? Why did Jesus succeed? How can you too succeed in serving God?

Lord Jesus, keep me from complaining about what I lack. Give me Your power to use what I have in Your service. Amen.

The Secret of Jesus' Power

BIBLE READING: *Mark 1:32-38*

It was a quiet night. The moonlight bathed the lake and made Capernaum sparkle like a jewel. But people in Capernaum were too excited for sleep. They had just lived through a day never to be forgotten.

For the first time they had heard Jesus, the young Prophet, preach in their synagog. Never had they heard a sermon like it. And before their very eyes they had seen Jesus heal a man by a simple command. Word spread that after the service Jesus also healed Peter's mother-in-law. So by evening people had come from far and wide to lay the sick in the street before Peter's house. And Peter's Houseguest came out and healed them.

"What is the secret of His power?" people wondered. They planned to go see Jesus in the morning and find out.

The sun had barely peeked over the hills when there was a knock at Peter's door. The sleepy Peter was greeted by people demanding, "We want to see Jesus!"

Peter went up to the roof to waken Jesus, but where was He? Peter woke the other disciples. No, they didn't know where Jesus was. In a few minutes Peter was leading the crowd up the hill behind the town to search for Jesus.

When the sun was well up in the sky, they found Jesus at last. And they discovered part of the secret of His power, for they found Him *praying*. Jesus always set aside time and found a place where He could be alone to talk with His Father.

The full secret of Jesus' power, of course, is that He is the Son of God. But when He lived in this world as a man, He did not always use His power as God. Instead He often depended on His Father in heaven for the power He needed. His Father always heard His prayers and gave Him such power. This power He is also ready to give to all who believe in Jesus.

Do you set aside time for prayer? Do you have a place where you can be alone with God? If not, you are missing out on the power God wants to give you.

Dear Jesus, teach me to pray as You prayed. And give me Your power to serve the Father and help people. Amen.

Jesus' Brothers and Sisters

BIBLE READING: *Mark 3:20-35*

Did you know Jesus had brothers and sisters? The Bible says so, though by "brothers and sisters" the Bible sometimes means "cousins." Who are Jesus' brothers and sisters? His cousins? Or who? To find out, let's go back to Capernaum, to the day of Jesus' homecoming.

Sometime earlier Jesus had left His home in Capernaum and together with His disciples had traveled about Galilee. On this trip Jesus had been the guest preacher in almost every synagog in Galilee. His words had stirred people. And His many miracles had startled them. "Where did He get all that power?" people asked.

"Probably from the devil," some answered. Even some of His old friends and neighbors thought so.

Everyone was curious. When Jesus returned to His home in Capernaum, people poured out of their houses to see their famous neighbor. Large numbers of people crowded around Jesus' house and peered in the windows. Jesus and His disciples couldn't even eat a meal in privacy.

Among the people who came to see Jesus were His mother and "brothers and sisters." But when they reached His house, they couldn't get through the crowd. So they passed the message from mouth to mouth until at last someone told Jesus, "Your mother and Your brothers and sisters are outside asking for You."

Jesus answered: "Who are My mother and brothers and sisters?" He gestured toward His disciples, who were sitting around Him. "Here are My mother and My brothers and sisters," He said. "Whoever does the will of God is My brother and sister and mother."

God's will is that we believe in Jesus as our Savior and Lord. Do you believe in Him? Then *you* are His brother or sister.

My Savior, because You are my Brother, I know Your home will be my home. Help me make my home also Your home. Amen.

Jesus' Own City

BIBLE READING: *Matthew 11:23-24*

From the north shore a lonely grove of trees juts out into the Sea of Galilee. Within this grove are some old ruins — all that's left of Capernaum, the city which the Bible calls Jesus' "own city." Why has Capernaum become nothing but a ruin?

When Jesus moved from unfriendly Nazareth, He made Capernaum His home. And He turned Capernaum into the most honored city in the world. In this city He preached more sermons, did more miracles, and healed more sick people than in any other city. And how often the people of Capernaum must have seen Him wave hello as He walked their streets!

Whenever Jesus finished traveling about the country, He returned to Capernaum. The people were always glad to see Him back. They remembered how He healed the centurion's servant and many others. They knew that any time they needed help they could depend on Jesus. Unlike Nazareth, here was a city that was proud to say, "Jesus lives here."

Jesus loved Capernaum and its people. Yet one day He said: "As for you, Capernaum, will you be exalted to the skies? No, brought down to the depths! For if the miracles had been performed in Sodom which were performed in you, Sodom would be standing to this day. But it will be more bearable, I tell you, for the land of Sodom on the day of judgment than for you." (NEB)

Why? Many people in Capernaum enjoyed having Jesus around. They liked His sermons and healings, but they didn't want to be His followers or turn from their sins. So instead of being saved, they fell under God's judgment.

Jesus is as popular and well liked by church people today as He was by the people of Capernaum. We have seen His love. We have experienced His forgiveness. And we know He lives among us. But are we willing to follow Him and turn from our sins? Or will we be like the people of Capernaum?

Lord Jesus, You have called us "Your own people." Give us the faith to live as Your people. Amen.

Childish People

BIBLE READING: *Luke 7:31-35*

As a boy Jesus must have seen many bamboo pipes. Perhaps He played music on one Himself. Many children made their own pipes. Maybe Jesus did too.

Perhaps as Jesus and His playmates were sitting in the marketplace one day, one boy began playing a merry tune on his pipes. "That gives me an idea," someone announced (maybe it was Jesus). "Let's play wedding. We can dance and sing to the pipes, like they do at real wedding parties."

"No, no," someone complained. "That's too happy and gay."

"Well," said the first, "let's play funeral then. We'll cry and wail to a sad tune, like they do at real funerals."

"No, no," another objected. "That's too sad."

Some children just didn't know what they wanted to do. So they did nothing and had a very dull time.

When Jesus was a grown man, He saw people act as childish as those children in the marketplace. They refused to believe the message of John the Baptist because, they said, he never seemed to have a good time. But they also refused to believe Jesus' message because, they said, He seemed to have too good a time.

168

Concerning these people Jesus said: "They are like children sitting in the marketplace and calling to one another, 'We piped to you, and you did not dance; we wailed, and you did not weep.'"

Do we sometimes act like childish people? Do we complain that we have nothing to do, yet say we don't have time to pray or have devotions or help people? Childish people always find excuses not to do God's will and then complain that life is dull.

Let's not be childish but childlike — trusting Jesus and doing whatever He calls us to do.

To think about: What is the difference between being childish and being childlike? Which are you?

Life is an exciting adventure, Lord, when I follow Your call. Help me answer yes to everything You want me to do. Amen.

You're Not Left Out

BIBLE READING: *John 14:1-3*

Have you ever taken a ride through a section of a city where rich people live? Maybe you said, "I wish I could live in a nice house like one of those."

Jesus' disciples must have had similar thoughts when they walked past the great palaces of the Herods in Tiberias, Jericho, and Jerusalem. Built in the Greek style, these palaces had many wings with long outdoor corridors. Each wing was surrounded by gardens and trees, pools and fountains. And in each wing were many small apartments, sometimes called mansions or rooms, reserved for special guests.

As Jesus and His disciples walked by, perhaps one of the disciples said, "Look at all those wonderful rooms."

"Lots and lots of rooms," another disciple might have answered, "but none for us. You have to be somebody real important to get an invitation to live there. They'll never have rooms for nobodies like us. We'll always be left out."

Maybe Jesus didn't say anything just then. But the night before He died Jesus noticed how sad and troubled His disciples were. He forgot His own troubles and told them: "In My Father's house are many rooms; if it were not so, would I have told you that I go to prepare a place for you?"

Jesus wanted His disciples and us to know that we are not nobodies. And we are not left out. All of us who believe in Him count big with God. He has a place specially prepared for each of us in His heavenly home. So instead of worrying about becoming rich or famous or important, we can think about helping other people who are less fortunate than we are. We're already so well taken care of that we can spend our time joyfully looking out for others.

To think about: In what ways are we who have Jesus far richer than those rich people who don't have Jesus?

Lord Jesus, by Your sacrifice You have prepared a place for me where You live and have brought joy into my life. By the sacrifices I make, help me share this joy with others. Amen.

What a Breakfast Said

BIBLE READING: *John 21:9-14*

On a rock-strewn stretch of shore by the Sea of Galilee is a large, flat rock. The Crusaders called it *mensa Christi,* or "the table of Christ." It reminds us of an incident that happened there almost 2,000 years ago.

The first rays of the morning sun began dissolving the mist that rose from the sea. A lone figure stood on the shore quietly fanning a charcoal fire. Through the vanishing mist He could see a fishing boat about a hundred yards out. "Catch anything yet?" He called out over the water.

"No," came the answer.

"Cast your net on the other side of the boat."

171

After a few minutes of silence there was lots of commotion in the boat. The fishermen grunted and strained to haul in the net now swarming with fish. "It's the Lord," whispered one fisherman. Then there was a splash as another fisherman plunged into the water and swam for shore.

The other six fishermen weren't in so big a hurry to reach shore. They too were eager to see Jesus again, but perhaps they still felt guilty. They remembered how they had deserted Jesus when He was arrested and crucified. They had seen Jesus twice since — on Easter and the Sunday after — and He had not scolded them. But they had seen Jesus only briefly then. Perhaps they thought, "This time we're in for it."

But when they reached shore, they were greeted by a smiling Jesus. "Come and have breakfast," He invited them. They saw that the Lord had fried some fish and baked some bread for them. Would He have done that for them if He were angry with them? No, He was still their Friend, and they knew they were forgiven.

When we've done something wrong and think Jesus can't possibly love us anymore, let's remember that breakfast by the sea. Jesus doesn't hold any grudges. He says: "I'm still your Friend. Won't you be My friend? Come, follow Me."

Lord Jesus, when my sins bother me, show me Your gentle and forgiving love as You did to Your disciples. Amen.

Far Removed from Galilee

BIBLE READING: *John 14:18-21*

Atop a green slope two shepherds pasture their flock of sheep and goats. Far beneath them sprawls the Sea of Galilee like a huge, deep-blue sapphire. The haze gives the rust-colored mountains beyond the sea a bluish tint. Here and there a white puff floats peacefully across the warm summer sky. And scattered about the rim of the lake are little clusters of white buildings — towns where Jesus once walked.

The whole scene must look just as it did when Jesus moved through these hills with His disciples. If only we could have been there then! If only we could have walked at His side, slept under the stars with Him, climbed these hills and eaten under the shade of the same tree with Him!

But now we live in a different land and a different time. Our streets are filled with the noise and exhaust fumes of cars. Our sleepy country roads have become superhighways, our lakes hidden behind billboards. Our alleys are littered with trash cans, and overhead scream the jets. Life seems so far removed from Galilee and Jesus.

Far removed from Galilee, yes; but from Jesus, no! Jesus said: "Lo, I am with you always" (Matthew 28:20). He is with us today as surely as He was with His disciples. In a crowded subway or towering skyscraper, in a run-down apartment or large country home, Jesus is with us. Wherever we eat or sleep, work or play, Jesus is beside us. Galilee is only the place where He lived long ago. Today He lives in Alberta and Alabama, Connecticut and California—where *you* live. He lives there so He can love you and forgive you and care for you. He'll live with you every moment until you come to live with Him forever.

To think about: Can you imagine Jesus flying in a jet, being in a school gym class or in a tree house? If you've been in these places, so has Jesus. How do you know that?

Lord, since You are my constant Companion, help me prove to be a true friend to You in all I do. Amen.

Tomb Decorators
BIBLE READING: *Matthew 23:29-35*

In the rocky hills surrounding Jerusalem one can see many man-made caves. These are tombs where the people who lived in Jerusalem long ago buried their dead. Most of the tombs look quite plain, having a simple doorway that is usually sealed shut by a large stone.

Here and there, though, one finds a tomb with a very fancy front. When Jesus visited Jerusalem, He saw many of these beautiful tombs. Many of them were tombs of prophets—men of God who had called on people of an earlier century to repent of their sins. A number of these prophets had been killed by people who hated the truth and didn't want to reform their lives.

The people who heard Jesus preach felt sorry these prophets had been murdered. Some said: "If we had been living when these prophets preached, we would have believed them and honored them." To prove this, they built fancy fronts on the prophets' tombs.

Jesus called some of these people "hypocrites" because they decorated the tombs of dead prophets but hated the prophets who were now living among them. Soon they would kill Jesus and some of His disciples. They were really no different from their forefathers who had killed the earlier prophets.

Are we guilty of such hypocrisy? We honor men of God who lived long ago, like Martin Luther, the great reformer. But while honoring such dead reformers do we dishonor the reformers living among us today? Do we disobey the Word of God our pastors teach us? Do we hate or ignore those who call on us to love and treat fairly those of another race? Do we get mad at those who tell us to share with the poor?

We honor God and His reformers of old when we listen to and follow God's reformers of today.

To think about: Through which persons you know has God called on you to reform your life? In what ways does your life need reforming? Do you really want God to reform your life?

Holy Spirit, remove all hypocrisy from my heart. Through Your Word help me reform my life. Amen.

What Eating an Apple Did

BIBLE READING: *1 Peter 3:8-12*

What do you do when someone says or does something nasty to you? Most people say or do something nasty in return.

Baseball player Don Demeter had a better idea. When he was playing outfield for the Detroit Tigers, an angry fan threw an apple at him. He could have thrown it back at the fan. Instead he picked up the apple and calmly began to eat it. Many people who had been angry with Don Demeter because he hadn't been playing too well suddenly cheered him.

The Bible says: "A soft answer turns away wrath, but a harsh word stirs up anger" (Proverbs 15:1). When we answer nastiness with nastiness, this seldom ends the matter. One harsh word only leads to another. But a "soft," or kind, answer often turns off people's anger and ends a fight before one can get started.

In today's Bible reading St. Peter tells us: "Do not return evil for evil or reviling [insults] for reviling; but on the contrary bless, for to this you have been called, that you may obtain a blessing." God has chosen us to receive the blessing of His forgiveness. And He calls on us to share that blessing with others.

When people crucified Jesus and then added their insults to His suffering, He prayed: "Father, forgive them; for they know not what they do" (Luke 23:34). When we today hurt Jesus by our disobedience, He doesn't try to get even with us but still prays: "Father, forgive them." This is the great blessing we have as God's children. Let's learn to share this blessing by forgiving those who wrong us.

To think about: How did Don Demeter "turn off" people's anger? How can you? What special reason do you have for doing so?

Merciful Lord, help me show forgiveness and kindness to those who hurt me. In this way I will be sharing the forgiveness and kindness You give me every day. Amen.

Like a Bulldog

BIBLE READING: *2 Timothy 2:1-6*

Americans often refer to George Washington as the father of their country. They call him this because he was their first President and, probably more important, he was the commander in chief of the American armies during the War of Independence.

Strangely enough, in many ways Washington was not a very good general. He lost almost every major battle he fought. The greatest American victories, like Saratoga, were won by other generals. Even Washington's final victory, at Yorktown, was won more by the French fleet and army than by Washington's army.

As a general Washington made many blunders. Some say his biggest was in making his soldiers fight British style — out in the open in long lines — rather than in the Indian style they were used to.

Why, then, do Americans consider Washington such a great general? Not because of his brilliance but because of his faithfulness to duty. He held his ragged army together in the most trying times and in the face of the greatest difficulties. Many far more capable generals have lost because they gave up when the going got tough. In the end Washington won because he just wouldn't give up.

George Washington can be an example to us as Christians. God may not have given us as much ability as He has given some others. But He has given us the

Holy Spirit, and by the Spirit's power we can be faithful to Christ. We can serve Him with bulldog determination no matter how rough the going, no matter how many people urge us to give up.

We too, then, shall win out in the end. Jesus promised: "Be faithful unto death, and I will give you the crown of life." (Revelation 2:10)

To think about: If you could choose between being brilliant or being faithful in serving Jesus, which would you choose? Why? How did Jesus show His faithfulness in serving us?

My Savior, make me faithful in serving You as You were faithful unto death in serving me. Amen.

A Quarter May Come Along

BIBLE READING: *Matthew 16:21-25*

Little Billy is looking for a quarter. That's because his big brother found a quarter the other day. Billy's brother must have walked the curb for 3 hours before he found the quarter. But he felt quite lucky. Sometimes when he goes walking the curb for money, he doesn't find a cent.

Well, how's little Billy making out? He hasn't found any money yet. How many blocks has he walked

so far? None. He's just going to keep on sitting by the curb here. He figures sooner or later a lost quarter is bound to come rolling his way.

Let's not laugh. He's too young to know better.

But we're not. So if we want to find ways to serve God and help people, we know better than to just sit back and wait for an opportunity to come rolling our way. Certainly that's not the way Jesus did it. He went looking for ways to serve God. He searched for people to help.

His search took Him all the way to the cross. The Scriptures made it clear that He would have to suffer and die if He wanted to save us. But Jesus didn't wait for suffering to find Him. He went looking for it. The Bible says: "Jesus began to show His disciples that He *must* go to Jerusalem and suffer many things . . . and be killed and on the third day be raised."

Now He calls on us whom He has saved to follow Him, to search as He did for ways to serve God. Our search will lead us deeper into the Bible. There we will find ways to serve God. In our schoolbooks we'll learn skills that will help us serve people. And in our churches and schools, neighborhoods and homes we will find plenty of chances to serve — if we're really looking for them.

But surely we are looking. How can we help it when we remember how Jesus went looking for ways to serve us?

To think about: In looking for ways to serve God do you search the way Billy searched or the way Jesus did? Where can you begin your search tomorrow?

Prayer suggestion: Ask the Lord to help you in your search for opportunities to serve Him and His people.

Barefoot over Burning Coals

BIBLE READING: *Romans 8:26-32*

Can you imagine anyone trying to bribe God?

In India some Hindus walk barefoot across red-hot coals. If you ask them why they do this, they explain they're trying to persuade God to answer their prayer. If their prayer is for only a little favor, they walk only a short distance on the burning coals. If their prayer is for a big favor, they walk a longer distance on the coals.

How foolish for anyone to think God needs some sort of bribe like that before He'll do us any favors! He loves nothing better than to answer our prayers. St. Paul writes: "He who did not spare His own Son but gave Him up for us all, will He not also give us all things with Him?" God has already given us His very best Gift—Jesus. Surely that proves He's ready and eager to give us whatever else is good for us.

If God doesn't always give us everything we pray for, it's not because He's waiting for some bribe. Rather it's because He knows that some of the things we pray for would really hurt us. He may see that a new bike would get us into an accident. And a larger allowance may lead us to forget Him as we start buying the things we've always wanted.

The gifts of the Spirit, such as forgiveness of sins and a more loving heart, God will always give us, because these are good for us. He'll also give us everything else that's really good for us. Why? Not because we've found some way to bribe Him but because we are His children through faith in Jesus.

To think about: Why is it foolish to think God needs to be bribed before He'll do us any favors? Why doesn't God give us everything we want? Why does He give us everything that is good for us?

Dear Father, how lucky I am to be Your child! You give me nothing but good — and far more than I deserve. Amen.

Junk or Treasure?

BIBLE READING: *Matthew 13:44-45*

There's a popular party game called "Treasure Hunt." Perhaps you've played it. It works like this: The group is divided into several teams. Each team gets a list of objects to hunt, like a chewing gum wrapper, a canceled 4-cent stamp, a rubber band, a bottle cap, a rusty screw. Each team hunts around the neighborhood until it finds all the objects on its list. The first team finished is the winner.

Imagine the thrill the winning team feels as it spreads out its "treasure" before the game's judges. Yet after all the time spent on the hunt, what is the "treasure" really worth? It's nothing but a pile of worthless junk.

How much like real life! We can be forever planning, scheming, saving, dreaming of how to get new treasures that we're sure will bring us happiness. But after we've gotten them, we find they don't keep us happy. They're junk after all.

When we were little, perhaps we wanted toys or dolls. Later perhaps we wanted a bike or new dress. But after we get these things, are we really satisfied? For a while maybe, but that's all. Somehow we always wind up wanting something more. Our newfound treasures just aren't treasures enough to keep us happy forever. After a while we're ready to cast them aside as junk.

Only one treasure can keep us happy forever. That treasure is Jesus. His love for us never wears out. His forgiveness is always new. The life He shares with us is always a challenging adventure.

If we have everything in the world except Jesus, we have nothing but junk. But even if we have nothing in the world except Jesus, we have the richest Treasure of all. So if you have a bike or new dress, go ahead and enjoy it. But don't expect too much of such things. They are not your real treasure. Jesus is.

To think about: Some people get no joy out of Jesus, because they ignore Him. Is this true of you? How much do you praise Him? talk to Him? learn about Him? serve Him?

Precious Jesus, sometimes I'm so tempted to spend all my time hunting junk and ignoring You. Help me realize that You alone are my true Treasure. Amen.

Who Are the Villains?

BIBLE READING: *Luke 22:39-51*

The mob that enters Gethsemane is armed. But the sleepy disciples are unsuspecting. After all, the mob is led by Judas, their friend and companion. See, Judas greets Jesus in the usual way and gives Him a kiss.

Hold on! The mob is surging forward to seize Jesus. Treachery! Betrayal! Now the disciples realize it. "Lord, shall we strike with the sword?" one calls out. Peter does not wait. Down his sword slashes on the villainous mob!

What thoughts must have flashed through the disciples' minds in that instant! Perhaps these words from Bach's *St. Matthew Passion* express what the disciples were thinking: "Loose Him! Hold it! Bind Him

185

not! O Hell, open your fiery pit! Consume them! Destroy with sudden fury the false betrayer, the murderous mob!"

Yes, Judas and the mob—*they* are the villains! *They* are causing Jesus' death! But wait! What power have they over Him whose command the invisible armies of heaven obey? By a mere word Jesus could strike down ten thousand armed mobs. But He doesn't. Instead He stops Peter's sword. For Jesus knows that the villains here are not just Judas and this mob. Peter too is a villain, as are all the disciples, and also we. By the wrongs we have done each of us has played the villain. We are the culprits who have caused Christ's death. We drove Jesus to the cross.

Jesus didn't fight it. He went meekly with the mob as a lamb to the slaughter so He could save the villains: Judas, the mob, the disciples, us. It was His Father's will. It was His own heart's desire. So He calmly accepted our betrayals and went out to die for them that He might forgive them.

> Lord, drops of grief can ne'er repay
> The debt of love I owe;
> Here, Lord, I give myself away,
> 'Tis all that I can do. Amen.

Poetic Justice

BIBLE READING: *Matthew 26:59-68*

The book *The Postman Always Rings Twice* tells a story of what we call "poetic justice." A man murders his wife, but the court declares him innocent. According to the law he can never again be tried for this crime. But later another court sentences him to death for a murder he never committed. Justice has its way after all.

Poetic justice overtook Jesus too. After His arrest He was tried before the Sanhedrin, the supreme court of His nation. Caiaphas, the high priest, had failed to prove Jesus guilty of any crime, for Jesus was completely without sin. But placing Jesus under oath, Caiaphas asked Him to testify whether or not He was the Son of God. Jesus answered, "Yes, I am."

The members of the court now had only two choices. They had to either accept His claim and worship Him as their Lord, or they had to sentence Him to death for blasphemy. It is blasphemy for any mere man to say he is God. Most of the members of the court didn't believe Jesus. So they pronounced their verdict: "He deserves death."

Jesus was sentenced to die for a crime He never committed. He was no blasphemer. He had spoken the simple truth. He *is* the Son of God. Yet here is the strange twist of poetic justice. Jesus was guilty of many other terrible crimes about which the Sanhedrin knew nothing.

Jesus was guilty of eating the forbidden fruit in Eden, of worshiping the golden calf, of beheading John the Baptist. In fact He was guilty of every sin that was committed from the beginning of time right down to the present. That includes our sins too, for God had transferred to Jesus the whole rotten load of all our sins. And for these crimes not the Sanhedrin but God Himself sentenced Jesus to die.

Why did God do it? So we might be declared innocent by heaven's court. Was there ever love like this? God sentences His Son to die for the likes of us! And for the likes of us Jesus accepts the sentence most willingly.

> Was it for crimes that I had done
> He groaned upon the tree?
> Amazing pity, grace unknown,
> And love beyond degree!

"Where Is His Body?"

BIBLE READING: *Mark 16:1-8*

It was Easter 1966. In Moscow a congregation of Christians walked in a procession around their church. As they walked, they looked this way and that, imitating the women of long ago who searched in vain for Jesus' body.

Suddenly a communist youth group showed up. They laughed at the Christians and shouted, "Jesus is dead! Jesus is dead!"

The Christians quietly continued their walk and search, as if to say, "But, then, where is His body?"

This is a good question. For almost 2,000 years some people have insisted that Jesus is dead. Yet not one of them has been able to find His dead body. And they never will, for Jesus has risen as the angels at His tomb declared.

Of course we know that Jesus is alive not simply because His body has never been found. This proves only that His body is missing. We know Jesus is alive because we see signs of His life everywhere. We see Him living in those Christians of Moscow who just will not give up their faith. We see Jesus alive in people who have turned from a life of selfishness to a life of love. And as we experience a love in our own lives that won't let us go, we know Jesus is alive in us.

St. Paul said of himself: "It is no longer I who live but Christ who lives in me" (Galatians 2:20). We can say the same. When we believe in Jesus, He is living in us, and our life isn't really ours but His. This is really good news.

Once Jesus' enemies found it easy to kill Him. That was when He was laying down His life for our sins. But He has risen from the dead. Now no one can kill Him. Because our life is really His life in us, we are alive forever. Not even our dying can change this fact. Jesus lives, and because He lives, so do we — now and forever!

To think about: What signs of Jesus' life do you find in you? What does Jesus' life in you mean for you?

Risen Lord, live in me with Your victorious power and endless love. And let the life I live be truly Your life in me. Amen.

Return of Herald the Angel

BIBLE READING: *2 Corinthians 11:12-15*

Hi! Don't be afraid. It's me, Herald the angel. Well, it's been quite a while, hasn't it? Want to take another tour with me? I've got some surprises to show you.

For our first stop I thought I'd take you to see the devil's top agent in your area. No, it's not Mr. Kuechenmeister. I know you think he's the meanest man around because he always yells at you. And true, the police have to arrest him every once in a while. But believe me, we angels know he's far from the worst.

Ah, here we are—the Red Cross blood bank. And there he is—Mr. Jaster, the nice-looking man over there donating a pint of blood. Surprised? He does lots of good things—collects money for the local hospital, coaches a Little League team, spends some of his free time helping the poor.

"What's so bad about that?" you ask. Nothing, except he does it all for the wrong reason. You see, he doesn't believe in God. And he goes around doing good to prove to people they don't need God or Jesus' forgiveness.

I suppose you always thought the devil made people do only "bad" things. No, he's too tricky for that. He sometimes disguises himself as "an angel of light." To trick people into not believing in Jesus, he often makes the bad guys look good and the good guys (God's people) look bad.

What can you do about Mr. Jaster? Tell people how bad he really is? No. Too often people try to do that sort of thing and end up picking on God's agents by mistake. The best thing for you to do is to make sure you don't fall for that other part of the devil's plan—to make the good guys look bad. For if you, a child of God, do evil things, you'll be helping the devil to make people think Jesus is evil too.

See you tomorrow?

To think about: Why does the devil at times get his people to do what seems to be good? Why does he want you to do bad things? Do you sometimes "fall for" his evil plans?

Lord Jesus, help my life lead people to You, not away from You. Amen.

Herald and the Poor

BIBLE READING: *Luke 16:19-25*

All set for another tour with an angel? Good. Two stops today. The first is a meeting over at the church.

Here we are. The men are discussing one man's suggestion—to give $100 a month to help support two poor families who live across town. Now listen to Mr. Jansen.

"I say no. People wouldn't be poor if they weren't so lazy. No one gives me any handouts. I've had to work hard for what I've got. Let the poor people do the same."

Well, enough of that. C'mon. Our next stop is the hospital.

Here we are—the maternity ward. Look through the nursery window. See all the newborn babies? They sure can cry! Well, several of them have something to cry about. They're going to be real poor. You know why? Because they're lazy? No. That *is* the reason *some* people are poor. But lots of people are poor for other reasons.

Take that chubby baby, for instance. He doesn't have the brains you have. No matter how hard he studies, he'll never make it past the fourth grade. He'll never get a good-paying job.

Or that one on the end. He's got very weak lungs. He'll never be able to do any heavy lifting or things like that. It would kill him. So he'll be poor. Oh, I know what you're thinking. No, he'll not be able to get a desk job either. You see, people won't hire him for a desk job because his skin is dark.

And that one over there. He's already got six brothers and sisters. His parents can barely afford to feed them. Now they have to feed him too. What's worse, he's got six more brothers and sisters to be born yet. So he'll have to quit school early to help support them. No, he'll never get a good job with so little education.

Well, these are only a few reasons people are poor. You weren't born with their problems. God's been extra good to you. So He wants you to be extra good to those who have such problems. And not like Mr. Jansen!

Lord, help me share with the poor what You have given me. I know You love them as You love me. Amen.

Herald and the Discouraged

BIBLE READING: *1 Kings 19:13-18*

Hello. It's Herald again. Want another peek at what we angels see? OK. Two stops again today.

First this youth meeting. See those two young men over there, one black and one white? They sure are discouraged, aren't they? Did you get the drift of what they were saying? "No one cares. No one's doing anything about the racial hate and injustice in our land."

C'mon now. I want to take you to meet someone. Here, just peek through the window. See that old man? He's a retired pastor. Did you know that for 40 years he told people that Jesus wants us to be fair and kind to everyone, no matter what their skin color?

Some members got mad at him. Others just ignored him. But some listened and did as the Lord wanted. I'd tell you the pastor's name, but you wouldn't recognize it. He's not famous in the civil rights movement. In fact he did his work before the civil rights movement began.

He never became well known for his success. But he did have *some* success. He planted seeds. And he wasn't the only one. Thousands of people were quietly planting the seeds of God's concern. You saw some of that seed before in those two young men. You saw it sprouting and shouting, "Nobody cares!"

Those two young men care, though. But they weren't born that way. They care because of people like this pastor who taught them to care. Trouble is, they've forgotten about the people who taught them. So they think they're all alone.

Someday you may feel that way, like you're the only one in the whole world who's still serving the Lord—like Elijah felt. But you're never alone. Jesus doesn't take any vacation. He keeps on working in the world and working through people, lots of people.

So don't get discouraged like those two young men. But be like them in one way: plug away at serving the Lord.

Thank You, Jesus, for the people who have taught me to care. And help me to show that I care by what I do. Amen.

Herald at the Parsonage

BIBLE READING: *John 20:24-29*

Good day. How have you liked your tour with an angel so far? Been surprised a few times? Well, today we're going to visit your pastor. I've got a real shocker for you.

There he is driving up to the parsonage now. When he gets out of the car, watch the look on his face.

There. Did you see it? How would you describe it? Worried? Troubled?

He's just spent several hours over at the hospital praying with Mr. and Mrs. Roth. He was praying for their son Jimmy. Did you know him? Well anyway, he was hit by a car. Jimmy's parents and pastor were praying he'd get well. Praying real hard! But about an hour ago Jimmy died.

His parents are still crying. Pastor tried to comfort them. And now—do you know what Pastor's doing right now? Hang on. He's doubting. He's thinking maybe God hasn't forgiven him his sins and that's why his prayer wasn't answered. Oh, you didn't know pastors sin? Sure they do. They need forgiveness just as you do. Only right now Pastor's doubting God's forgiveness.

Are you shocked? You shouldn't be. Pastors sometimes have doubts just like everyone else—like you, maybe. You see, the devil works on everyone, even pastors. But don't be upset. The Holy Spirit is also working on your pastor. He'll snap him out of it. In fact He'll make Pastor's faith stronger than it was before.

Remember how Jesus helped St. Thomas over his doubts? Well, He's going to help your pastor too. The next time your pastor sees Mr. and Mrs. Roth, they'll remind him of what we angels know: Jimmy is very happy now.

When you have doubts, remember you're not the only one. And God doesn't give up on you because you have doubts. Instead He steps in and helps you get over them and even makes your faith stronger. You see, God loves you far more than you can imagine.

196

To think about: How do you know God forgives even people's doubts?

Lord Jesus, thank You for not letting go of me even when I'm ready to let go of You. Amen.

Herald at the Publishers

BIBLE READING: *Isaiah 52:3-7*

I'm back. Herald at your service. Ready for a lightning tour? OK. But first I'd better explain the reason for today's trip.

We angels noticed you weren't too happy about getting up for Sunday school and church several weeks ago. In fact we read a question forming on the edge of your mind. You came close to asking, "Why can't I be a Christian all by myself? I could just read the Bible and my Sunday school lesson at home and not have to worship or study with others."

Today's trip is to help you answer that question. We're headed for a distant city. Wow, that was quick.

See this big building? It's the place where they write and print your Sunday school lessons. C'mon in. Look at all those printing presses and all those people — hundreds of them. Wow, it's noisy. Let's go up to the top floor.

See all these offices? The men and women who work here write your Sunday school lessons. And look at all the secretaries and artists! Did you know you needed so many people to provide you with Sunday school lessons? And you need lots more people than you see here.

For instance, that man writing your lessons. How do you suppose he learned so much about the Bible? He learned it from other Christians who taught him in school. And he learned it from books written by still other Christians.

You see why you can't be a Christian just by yourself? You need your Bible and lesson books. But you wouldn't have these without other Christians: the printers, the writers, the men who taught the writers in school or through books, and thousands of Christians who give their dimes and dollars to help pay for all this.

I could show you lots of other Christians you need. But I've got to get you back. Just remember: You need other Christians far more than you realize—even Christians who are already dead. But I'll tell you more about that tomorrow. OK?

Dear God, help me realize how much I need the other Christians You've placed around me to help me. Amen.

Herald in the Past

BIBLE READING: *Revelation 7:13-17*

Hi. It's Herald the angel again. Remember what I told you yesterday, that to be a Christian you need the help even of Christians who are already dead? It's true. I'll show you what I mean. Today we're going to take a trip back in time.

Hold on! Here we go—500, 1,000, 1,600, 1,667 years. We're in the year 303. See that Roman soldier? Listen as he reads to the townspeople.

"By decree of his majesty, Diocletian, Emperor of Rome, all Christian churches are to be burned to the ground. And anyone having a copy of the Scriptures shall surrender it to be burned. Anyone failing to do so will be put to death."

See those two men over there? They're Christians, but they're afraid. They're going to go home, get their copies of the Bible, and turn them over to the Roman soldiers. They know their Bibles will be burned, but they'd rather have that than be burned themselves.

Now see that girl over there? She too has a Bible, but she's going to hide it. I hate to tell you this, but somebody's going to report her. She'll be arrested. And the soldiers will torture her to find out where she's hidden it. But she won't tell. She'll die without telling.

Well, let's get back. Yes, you're right. She's brave, very brave. Ah, here we are—in the 20th century.

Do you realize that if it weren't for Christians like that girl you wouldn't have a Bible today to read? All Bibles would have been burned long ago. So you see, you really can't be a Christian all by yourself. You need other Christians. Without the other Christians of long ago and of today you wouldn't even know about Jesus and His salvation.

Yes, you need other Christians, and just as important, they need you. But let me tell you about that tomorrow. See you then?

Father in heaven, thank You for the many heroes of faith through whom You have brought the Gospel of Jesus to me. Amen.

Herald and the Empty Seats

BIBLE READING: *Philippians 2:1-4*

All set for another tour? Glad you're not afraid of an angel. Well, today we visit a church. Remember what I told you yesterday? That you can't be a Christian all by yourself because other people need you? C'mon, that's what I want to show you.

Here we are. This is a Wednesday evening church service. See that teen-age girl over there? You can't miss her. Only five other people are here. Look at all those empty seats!

Well, in spite of the very small attendance, the pastor just finished preaching a very fine sermon. But Miss Young—that's the girl's name—was laughing to herself all the way through the sermon. She was laughing at herself and asking, "What on earth did I come here for?"

You know why she came? Because she was having problems and hoped maybe God could help her. But let me tell you: She didn't come to hear the Word of God. She wasn't ready for that yet. Maybe she would have listened to it several weeks from now. But this time she came to observe. She wanted to see if Christians acted as if God were helping them. If they did, she thought she might ask God to help her too.

But what did she see? Mostly empty seats! So many Christians had stayed home or had gone other places. You know what Miss Young told herself? "Those Christians don't believe God helps them. If they did, they'd be here worshiping Him. I guess God doesn't help people. I was stupid to waste my time coming here."

You know, she may never be back. And I can assure you the angels in heaven are pretty sad tonight. And Jesus is pretty hurt. It could have turned out differently if only more Christians had been here. Just remember, other people do need you. They need to see you praising God for His goodness. It gives them just the encouragement they need. So be glad when church time rolls around.

Lord, help me worship You together with others so I can encourage them in their faith, for Jesus' sake. Amen.

Herald and Stubborn Love

BIBLE READING: *Revelation 2:10-11*

Hi. It's Herald again. Another angel told me I have to get back to my regular duties, so we'll have to make this our last visit. Today I thought I'd take you to see a Christian die. Oh, come on, don't get scared! This is something you really should know about because someday it'll probably happen to you.

I could take you to a local hospital, but most of the dying people there are so doped up by medicine they don't know what's happening. So here we go—far across the ocean. And here we are. Recognize the place? Yes, it's a war zone. Let's go inside that first-aid station.

See the soldier on that stretcher by the door? He was just brought in badly wounded. He's dying, and he knows it. Now look at his face. What do you see?

Pain? Yes. Anything else? Fear? Right again. Does that surprise you? You thought Christians aren't afraid of death? Well, you're right about one thing. Christians have no *need* to fear death. If you could see what we angels see—what wonderful things Jesus has prepared for His people—you'd see why.

But I'll tell you something else. We angels have seen millions of Christians die during the past two thousand years, and most of them have been afraid. In a way I don't blame any of them. Death isn't God's idea. It's the fault of sin and the devil.

Look at the soldier again. Notice, he's not as afraid anymore. He's remembering that Jesus died for Him and rose from the dead. He's remembering Jesus' promise of eternal life. He's still a bit nervous, but he's in good hands. He'll soon be with Jesus.

I wanted you to see this because you may get scared when you're dying. I hope not. But if you do, don't think Jesus will get mad and let the devil have you. Oh, no! Jesus went through this dying business Himself so He could turn your dying into a great and glorious victory. And if you think He'll let a little fear on your part keep Him from giving you His victory, you don't know how "stubbornly" He loves you.

Lord Jesus, share with me Your victory. Amen.

Index of Bible Readings

NOTE: The boldface numbers are devotion numbers

Lev. 19:32; **34**

Deut. 33:26-29; **3**

1 Kings 19:13-18; **105**

Ps. 1; **36**

Ps. 8; **77**

Ps. 47; **42**

Ps. 84; **8**

Ps. 85; **47**

Ps. 117; **18**

Ps. 139:13-18; **43**

Ps. 147:7-18; **29**

Is. 9:6-7; **69**

Is. 40:27-31; **4**

Is. 52:3-7; **107**

Is. 53; **46**

Jonah 3:10 – 4:11; **10**

Matt. 1:18-25; **63**

Matt. 5:43-48; **74**

Matt. 6:1-4; **38**

Matt. 6:7-8; **65**

Matt. 6:7-13; **20**

Matt. 10:29-31; **14**

Matt. 11:23-24; **89**

Matt. 13:31-32; **37**

Matt. 13:44-45; **99**

Matt. 15:10-20; **75**

Matt. 16:21-25; **97**

Matt. 16:24-27; **23**

Matt. 18:21-35; **33**

Matt. 20:25-28; **1**

Matt. 23:29-35; **94**

Matt. 25:1-13; **7**

Matt. 25:31-40; **24**

Matt. 25:31-46; **64**

Matt. 26:26-28; **45**

Matt. 26:59-68; **101**

Mark 1:32-38; **87**

Mark 3:20-35; **88**

Mark 16:1-8; **102**

Luke 1:67-75; **68**

Luke 1:76-79; **61**

Luke 2:1-7; **67**

Luke 6:37-38; **49**

Luke 6:41-42; **48**

Luke 7:31-35; **90**

Luke 11:27-28; **44**

Luke 16:19-25; **104**

Luke 16:19-31; **54**

Luke 21:25-28; **66**

Luke 22:39-51; **100**

Luke 24:45-53; **83**

John 1:9-14; **21**

John 1:14-18; **73**

John 1:43-46; **86**

John 14:1-3; **91**

John 14:12-14; **51**

John 14:18-21; **93**

John 15:12-17; **17**

John 20:24-29; **106**

John 21:9-14; **92**

Acts 1:9-12; **82**

Acts 28:1-10; **80**

Rom. 8:18-25; **52**

Rom. 8:26-32; **98**

Rom. 11:36; **57**

Rom. 15:1-3; **84**

1 Cor. 8:6; **55**

1 Cor. 10:13; **15**

1 Cor. 12:4-11; **72**

1 Cor. 15:35-50; **31**

1 Cor. 15:58; **41**

2 Cor. 3:1-3; **62**

2 Cor. 5:10; **81**

2 Cor. 5:14-21; **28**

2 Cor. 6:1-2; **85**

2 Cor. 11:12-15; **103**

Gal. 3:10-14; **59**

Gal. 5:16-26; **26**

Gal. 6:7-8; **71**

Eph. 4:22-32; **27**

Eph. 5:1-2; **25**

Eph. 5:17-20; **53**

Eph. 6:10-13; **30**

Phil. 2:1-4; **109**

Phil. 2:14-16; **60**

Phil. 4:4-7; **2**

Col. 1:9-14; **22**

Col. 1:15-20; **56**

1 Thess. 5:9-11; **16**

1 Tim. 2:1-4; **40**

1 Tim. 4:11-16; **50**

1 Tim. 6:6-11; **12**

1 Tim. 6:11-12; **78**

2 Tim. 2:1-6; **96**
2 Tim. 3:14-17; **79**
Heb. 10:22-25; **76**
Heb. 12:1-3; **11**
Heb. 12:5-11; **9**
Heb. 13:1-3; **39**

James 1:22-27; **70**
1 Peter 3:8-12; **95**
2 Peter 1:19-21; **13**
1 John 3:11-18; **19**
1 John 3:16-18; **5**
1 John 4:20-21; **58**

1 John 5:1-5; **6**
Rev. 2:10-11; **32**
and **110**
Rev. 7:13-17; **108**
Rev. 21:9-21; **35**